antiques on the cheap

A Savvy Dealer's Tips:
Buying ▸ Restoring ▸ Selling

James W. McKenzie

STOREY

Pownal, Vermont 05261

*The mission of Storey Communications is to serve our customers
by publishing practical information that encourages
personal independence in harmony with the environment.*

Edited by Deborah Balmuth and Marie Salter
Cover design by Meredith Maker
Cover photography copyright © Eric Roth Photography, of bureau owned
by Harry Zeltzer, Ipswich, MA
Text design and production by Susan Bernier
Production assistance by Eileen Clawson
Illustrations, except those on pp. 15, 19, 23, 33, 35, 39, 46, 47, 51, 58, 62,
65, 119, 178, and 186, by Robert Strimban
Indexed by Barbara Hagerty

Printed in the United States by Vicks Lithograph
10 9 8 7 6 5 4 3 2 1

Library of Congress Cataloging-in-Publication Data

McKenzie, James W. (James William), 1943–
     Antiques on the cheap: a savvy dealer's tips on buying, restoring, and
selling / James W. McKenzie.
          p.   cm.
          Includes index.
          ISBN 1-58017-073-0 (pb. : alk. paper)
          1. Antiques—Purchasing.   2. Antiques—Repairing.   3. Selling—Antiques.
          I. Title
     NK 1125.M3515   1998
     745.1'028—dc21   98-12316
                                                                              CIP

table of contents

dedication

*To my wife, Wanda, who is my partner, helper, loving
(and loved) constant companion, and "third hand,"
who tolerates a dining room full of pottery,
a garage filled with antiques, and a basement
that she's afraid to even look at.*

To Susan, who shares my love of things old.

To Dianne, who gives me grandbabies to love.

*To my grandchildren, Allison, Daniel, and Dennis,
who make me stop and play.*

introduction

Let's get something out of the way right up front. This is not just another antiques identification book, price guide, or refinishing manual. It isn't going to make you an expert on antiques or collectibles overnight, and, if you buy it, it's not going to make you rich or even good-looking. Oh, and there's another thing it isn't: a book for antiques dealers only.

What exactly is it, then? In short, it's the author's knowledge of buying, improving, and selling antiques and collectibles, gained through years of experience, and condensed into the simplest terms possible.

Who's This Book For?

It's a book for those of you who want to become dealers. It's also a book for people who have no interest in selling, but who like the idea of obtaining antiques at reasonable prices. And it's the perfect how-to for the folks who want to improve their finds with a minimum expenditure of time, effort, and money.

If you think that you, and just about everyone you know, fits that description, you're right. Interior decorators, people furnishing a home on a budget, bed-and-breakfast operators, and everyone else who likes old stuff will appreciate the information provided here.

By mastering a few of the tricks discussed throughout the book, even the longtime dealers among you can begin improving your profit margins. You should understand that this book is not really aimed at the dealers who can spend thousands of dollars on fine antiques and can afford to hold their purchases indefinitely before selling them at large profits. Chances are, those guys aren't out there looking for a book to tell them how to make money, anyway.

Primarily, the advice and information imparted here are intended to allow those of you with more modest means and limited expertise an avenue of acquiring some additional income while enjoying an interesting and rewarding occupation. If your time is limited, if you want to start out small or only work in the business part time, then this book is ideal for you.

1

If you don't want — or can't afford — to go out and buy a lot of expensive, specialized tools, then this book is for you. If you get a lot of satisfaction out of reaping the rewards of your own cleverness and efforts, then this book is for you. If you don't mind getting your hands a little dirty, then this book is definitely for you.

Tricks of the Trade

All craftsmen, tradesmen, or specialists in any business have tricks of the trade that they rely on to make their product more desirable or more salable, to make their jobs easier and their time more productive or profitable. Many of these so-called tricks are simple techniques learned through trial and error. Sometimes they're bits of information passed along by word of mouth, usually to a select few. Many are closely guarded secrets, jealously hoarded once learned.

Why is this information so closely guarded? Because in many cases it was so hard to come by in the first place, and because sometimes the technique or knowledge is a moneymaker. It's the old law of supply and demand. In theory, the fewer who know, the more money those in the know can make.

Still, the tricks that you'll learn in this book are not tricks in the sense that they are intended to dupe someone. You will *not* learn how to fake antiques.

What you will learn are techniques that will make what you sell more attractive and easier to sell. It will prepare you to be able to buy, at lower cost, the things that many dealers pass up because they don't know how to repair, replace, touch up, refinish, clean, display, or market what they have purchased.

Throughout this book you will find practical advice — advice that works for the author. Not everything will work as well for everyone. Regional differences make for differences in tastes. So while oak, for instance, sells well in one part of the country, perhaps it can't be given away in another.

As you'll discover, the overriding theme of this book is one of cost saving. Because of that fact, many of the processes and techniques prescribed are downright unorthodox.

The next most obvious concept underlying most of the advice you'll get here is the idea that a lot can be accomplished quickly without sacrificing good results. It's still true that time is money. Some things you do in the antiques business bring in relatively little money, so it's essential that you spend as little time on those projects as possible. The nice thing is that those little things add up.

The Method to This Madness?

You're not going to have to stumble blindly through this volume. There is some logical sequence to it. Since it's hoped that this book will be used as somewhat of a reference manual, it's understood that you'll need to locate information about different topics with relative ease. Therefore, the book has been divided into four parts:

1. **Buying.** Here's where you'll find all the author's favorite tricks for obtaining good things cheap — unless it can be had for nothing, that is. That's included, too.
2. **Improving.** This section is loaded with innovative tips for enhancing your acquisitions. The author made all the mistakes first, so you won't have to. You'd have to take several courses — or buy a lot of specialty books — to get these goodies.
3. **Fixing.** There's no doubt about it, if you can repair something that's broken, you'll have a tremendous advantage over most people. Lots of repairs are simple, and this part of the book will prove it.
4. **Selling.** So you've got all this stuff, now how do you get rid of it? More importantly, how do you turn it over quickly for a profit? There's a lot more to selling than just dumping your merchandise in a shop. Don't overlook this important step.

Have Fun!

It's the opinion of the author that if you can't have fun in this business, you ought not to be in it. The same can be said for this book, so everything possible has been done to make it entertaining as well as informative.

Let The World's Cheapest Antiques Dealer show you a few tricks!

RESTORE RESPONSIBLY

Some projects in the chapters that follow require harsh abrasives and chemicals. Be sure to read, understand, and follow the manufacturers' instructions and cautions before using such products. Also, check with your local sanitation department for approved disposal methods before disposing of any potentially toxic wastes.

---

buying

For me, this is the best part of being in the antiques business. I enjoy the search as much as, if not more than, the find. If I weren't selling antiques, I would still be out there looking for them. The problem is, if I weren't in the business, I would have to severely limit my purchases. So you might say that being a dealer justifies my insatiable desire to shop for antiques.

In fact, for many people, becoming an antiques dealer is usually a result of having acquired too much. Many collectors become dealers out of necessity. Their collections have outgrown the space they have to keep them in.

It seems that just about everyone who really loves antiquing is either a dealer now, has been a dealer in the past, or is thinking of becoming a dealer soon.

If you've made that transition, or are approaching it, or even if you *never* decide to go from just buying to buying for resale, you still need to make the best deals possible.

Getting into the antiques and collectibles trade is easier than it has ever been. Staying in business is as difficult as ever, or even more so. With the proliferation of group shops and "antiques malls," you've got to be competitive. And that means acquiring the merchandise and supplies you need at the lowest possible prices. Sometimes, you'll see, that even means for free.

That's what this part of the book is going to do for you. It's going to turn you into a shrewd dealer. If not a dealer, then at least a knowledgeable buyer. Are you ready to go shopping with The World's Cheapest Antiques Dealer?

taking the mystery out of auctions

Auctions are a lot of fun and a great place to buy antiques for resale. They're a lot more than that, though. An auction is also a game: a contest in which there are winners and losers. If you'd like to be one of the winners and have fun, there are some things you need know. First, auctions are addictive. Some people just can't see the sense in standing around all day waiting for one or two pieces to come up for bid. They find it excruciatingly boring. Others just can't stay away from auctions. Sometimes I go to one of these sales and don't spend a dime. That's pretty cheap entertainment, though, don't you think? To tell you the truth, I'm not sure if I go to auctions because I'm in the antiques business or if I'm in the antiques business as an excuse to attend auctions.

Types of Auctions

There are two types of auctions at which you can purchase antiques and collectibles: estate sales and consignment sales. It's not always easy to know which is which, though. In general, most estate sales are held at the home and include everything from the furniture to the contents of the kitchen cabinets. They are held to liquidate an estate so that the proceeds can be disbursed to the heirs.

Consignment sales, on the other hand, usually take place at an auction house that holds sales on a regular basis. Items from many different sources are consigned to the auction house for sale at a commission.

I don't like to recommend one type of auction over the other; I attend both on a regular basis. I do have my personal preference, however, and you'll soon develop your own. There are some subtle differences that you should be aware of, though.

5

Estate Sales

For the most part, at estate sales, with the possible exception of the real estate, everything will be sold with *no reserve*. This simply means that regardless of how low the bid is, the item will be sold to the highest bidder; there is no bottom price set by the owners or the auctioneer. Of course the auctioneer will attempt to get the highest price possible (that's his job), but he must move on to the next item. He can't dwell on a single piece.

Bidding Against Dealers

Now is a good time to dispel one of the most persistent misconceptions about auctions. Time and again I have heard people say, "Oh, no! There's a bunch of antiques dealers here. I can't compete against them."

Actually, nothing could be further from the truth. Remember, you're an antiques dealer, too. Or you should at least think like one. What are you willing to pay? If you're willing to pay more than wholesale, then you're in the wrong business.

Follow the Leader

If you're new at it, it's not a bad idea to go to a few auctions and familiarize yourself with the faces there. You'll soon begin to recognize the regulars, most of whom will be dealers, among the crowd. There's no guarantee that all dealers know what they're doing, but those who buy consistently and show up at a lot of sales are probably selling a lot and making a profit.

Until you get the hang of it, try to follow their lead. Don't be afraid to top their bids. After all, someone has to be the high bidder, and the knowledgeable dealers are going to keep the prices within the wholesale range.

READ THE AD

Most auctioneers who have permanent auction houses also do estate sales and sometimes move the entire estate to their establishment. Lack of adequate parking space at the site or inclement weather might prompt such a move, so read the ads carefully to know which type of auction you're attending.

Don't Get Carried Away

The chances are that another item just like the one you're bidding on will be in the next auction. And there are plenty of auctions to attend. Learn to divorce yourself from your personal likes and dislikes. When you're bidding on something, see it as merchandise. Calculate the possible profit even before you buy it. If you let your emotions take over, you tend to be willing to pay closer to what you would if you were buying from a shop at retail.

Beware the Bidding Wars

So now that we've established that dealers are cheap, who is it that you should not bid against? At many estate auctions, family members will be vying for family heirlooms. Maybe the will doesn't distribute these items or the relatives just can't get together on who gets what. In any case, there's no logic involved in this type of bidding.

Feuding siblings, for example, might clash in a battle of bidding that ends in one paying an exorbitant price for some cherished keepsake, just to keep it out of the hands of the other. Remember, in their own minds, these people aren't dealing in *real* money. Since the proceeds of the sale are going to be distributed among them, these purchases are simply going to reduce their share. In other words, it's not "out of pocket."

You'll learn to recognize these bidding wars. Take care not to get sucked into one. It's easy to assume that just because a number of people are willing to pay a big price for something, the object is of great value.

If you suspect a bidding war, wander around and talk to people. Someone will know who the family members are. They'll probably even want to fill you in on who doesn't get along with whom.

All this isn't intended to scare you away from estate auctions. And you shouldn't be afraid to bid by any means. Ninety-nine percent of the stuff at these auctions is of no sentimental value to the heirs. In fact, they're tickled to death to see it sold.

Establish the Provenance

"Provenance" is just a fancy term for the origin of something. Once you've made a purchase at an estate sale, it's a good idea to try to get some of the history behind it. Where did it come from? How old is it? Many times, a relative of the deceased or even an old family friend can furnish some really interesting details. When you sell it, your customers will appreciate this kind of information. It makes the object less impersonal and can increase its worth, especially if the family has a history in the area.

I've Just Gotta Have That!

In my experience, there's another type of bidder who makes it difficult to purchase things "wholesale" at an auction: the ones who really want an item for themselves. They aren't going to sell it, and they just

---

GRANDPA NEVER LOOKED THAT GOOD

At one farm sale I attended, I got in on the bidding for a portrait in a mediocre frame. I estimated the frame's worth at about twenty dollars. When it reached that figure, I dropped out.

The bidding escalated: thirty dollars, forty dollars, one hundred dollars. It was obvious to me, and to most of the others there, what was going on. But a few novices had been caught up in the frenzy for a while.

In this case they were lucky and didn't get caught. The quarreling cousins were determined to duke it out with dollars. At four thousand dollars, the war ended. We'll never know who got the most satisfaction out of the purchase — the winning bidder or the one who successfully drove the price up to an absurd level. In any case, I'll bet those two are still not speaking to each other.

---

have to have it. They fawn over it throughout the auction and say things like, "Isn't it beautiful? I'd just love to own this."

Dealers, however, try their darnedest to show as little interest as possible. If they want something badly, they say things like, "Needs a lot of work. I had one just like this in my shop and it took me two years to sell the thing."

Of course, you can reverse the ruse — and possibly chase off a few bidders — by letting them "overhear" you talking about how you're going to buy this or that at any price. It's a crude tactic, but sometimes you can get away with it.

It's downright funny. We dealers are all there for the same thing — to buy! And, when we get there, we go around trying to convince each other that there's nothing there worth buying.

The most dreaded sight to a group of dealers is that of a young, excited couple. They won't bid on a great many things, but when they get to that one special item, watch out! Just back off and let them buy it.

Consignment Auctions

A lot of what I've said about the types of bidders you'll encounter applies to both estate and consignment sales. There are a few peculiarities of consignment sales that you should be alerted to, however. The rules change a bit in this version of the "game."

Why Was It Consigned?

Merchandise at a consignment sale is there for one of four reasons:
1. Someone bought it, cleaned it up, repaired or refinished it, and now intends to make a profit on it.
2. Someone needs the money or no longer needs the item.
3. It's been in a shop too long and consigning it is a sure sale, even if it's at a loss.
4. The auctioneer owns it, and this is one of his sources of income.

Who's in Control?

The nature of a consignment sale is such that considerable control can be exercised over the price at which an item sells. For instance, if the auctioneer owns it, he might decide not to sell a piece if the bidding isn't as high as he would like. He has this prerogative unless he has stated or advertised that everything will be sold with no reserve.

Often, rather than simply withdrawing an item, the auctioneer will bid on it himself. He probably won't announce that he's bidding, though. More than likely he will use a "house" number. If the bidding doesn't suit him, he might give the appearance that he's taking bids from the crowd and "sell" the item to the house number.

Also, it's not uncommon for a consignor to attempt to control the bidding. Since you won't know who has consigned what, one of your fellow bidders might, in fact, be the owner of the item on the block at the moment. It's possible for this ploy to backfire, however, with the owner being the final bidder and getting stuck with his own merchandise. This might be preferable to selling it too cheaply, though. The auctioneer will still be paid his commission, which can run 10 or 15 percent of the selling price.

Doctored Merchandise

Aside from the aforementioned practices, you should be on the alert for "doctored" merchandise that sometimes makes its way into consignment sales. I once bought a pie safe that had been painted an unattractive blue. I got it pretty cheap, thinking that, once stripped, it would be a great piece. When I was loading it on the truck, I didn't like the feel of the sharp edges on the bottom. When I got it home, my worst fears were realized.

Basically, only the doors and the top were original. All the rest was new wood. It had fooled me, but it wouldn't have if I had looked it over more carefully before bidding. I just got excited, thinking I was getting a good buy. This piece of furniture had been disguised by someone counting on my type of reaction.

Beware of "doctored" pieces
that look good from a distance.

What Are You Looking For?

Aside from the obvious need to see what's available, you should be looking at the overall quality of the merchandise. When examining glassware and ceramics, look for cracks, chips, flakes, and repairs. Unless your eyes are a lot better than mine, you'll miss some of these defects unless you carefully run your hands over the piece.

Where a good auctioneer will point out these flaws, they still can be missed or their severity understated. You might not consider yourself an expert, but you certainly know what you want in your shop or home.

Do We Need Counseling?

In addition to the more obviously damaged or doctored goods that you should be on the lookout for, bad "marriages" are also something to be wary of. Now I'm not talking about what can happen to your domestic situation if you spend too much time or money at auctions. In the language of antiques lovers, a piece of furniture that has been married is one that's been assembled from the parts of two or more similar pieces — for example, a marble top that doesn't quite conform in shape to the table that it sits on, or a mirror that doesn't seem to match the dresser it's paired with.

Having said all that, you might get the impression that I'm trying to scare you away from consignment auctions. Actually that's not the case. I've made many really good buys at these sales, and by exercising reasonable caution, you can, too. Most people in this business are honest and the vast majority of auctioneers are reputable; they strive to run their sales with fairness and integrity. But since there are a few unscrupulous people in this business, as in any enterprise, being forewarned is being forearmed.

I don't mean to overload you with too much information, and I certainly don't want to take all the fun out of going to auctions. But for many of you who intend to engage in the antiques trade, this will become your primary source for acquiring merchandise. For that reason, I feel that the subject deserves a little more attention. Here are a few more tricks to help you along.

Absentee Bidding

Don't feel that you have to sit there all day waiting to bid on one or two items that you're really interested in. At most auctions you can leave what is known as an *absentee bid*. This simply means that you decide what your maximum bid will be, and leave it with the auctioneer or an assistant. Your bid amount won't be announced when the object comes up, but if your bid is higher than the others, you'll get the item for whatever the next increment would be. Often this will be less than your

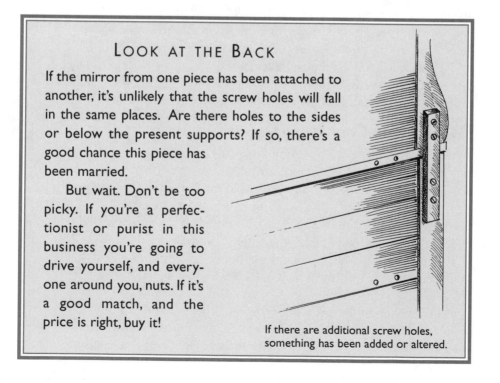

LOOK AT THE BACK

If the mirror from one piece has been attached to another, it's unlikely that the screw holes will fall in the same places. Are there holes to the sides or below the present supports? If so, there's a good chance this piece has been married.

But wait. Don't be too picky. If you're a perfectionist or purist in this business you're going to drive yourself, and everyone around you, nuts. If it's a good match, and the price is right, buy it!

If there are additional screw holes, something has been added or altered.

actual bid. Naturally you'll have to find out what the auctioneer's policies are regarding pickup and payment for your absentee purchase.

I use this method when there are a couple of auctions going on at the same time. I visit one, leave a few bids, and then check out the next sale. I might choose to stay at that auction, or, if the first seemed more interesting, leave bids at the second and return to the first.

But watch your budget! When you're hopping around from sale to sale, leaving a trail of absentee bids, you can easily end up spending money at two places simultaneously. My wife says that when I do this I am the epitome of the "ultimate auction addict." She's right, of course.

Bidding Strategies

Everyone seems to have a favorite bidding strategy, and every book I've read that mentions auctions seems to contradict the one before it. No doubt, as you gain experience, you'll develop the strategy that works best for you. But assuming that you're a novice, there are some rules of thumb that, if followed, will keep you from paying too much until you get the hang of it.

Don't Be First

The first and most obvious rule is: Never jump in when the auctioneer opens the bidding. This will sound pretty elementary to some of you. But many times I've seen inexperienced buyers raise their hands on the first figure the auctioneer mentions. There's nowhere to go but up from there. Usually there's a stunned silence with little, if any, further bidding. As a rule, auctioneers try to start the bidding at a figure somewhere around what he would like to get, if not a little higher. When no one responds, he drops the price until someone in the crowd opens the bidding.

Don't Even Be Second

I don't even recommend getting in immediately after the price "bottoms out." Why add yours to the escalating bids? Wait until the bidding appears to have stopped. There's plenty of time to get in then, if the price is still within your limit. The auctioneer will usually try to squeeze a little more out of the crowd. He'll normally indicate in some manner when the object is about to be sold. Don't expect that old "going once, going twice" routine, though. Every auctioneer is an individual, and each has his own method. Pay attention to how the auctioneer at each sale announces his intent to "knock the item down."

Sometimes auctioneers will end the bidding unexpectedly and catch you by surprise. It might even be their way of teaching late bidders that they should join in sooner. They don't particularly like bidders to wait until the last moment. Of course, if we always tried to keep the auctioneer happy, we'd all be broke.

Don't Scratch Your Nose

Don't rub your ear, wave to a friend, or nod your head at an auction. If we paid attention to this old warning, a crowd at an auction would look like a room full of department store mannequins. Actually, we're a pretty animated group, normally. But some newcomers may be afraid that if they make a sudden move, the auctioneer will misinterpret it as a bid, and they'll be stuck with something they really don't want. Understandably, folks new to auctions may seem a little cautious, but take heart!

SHOCK BIDDING

As I'm sometimes wont to do, I'll now contradict myself. There's a bidding tactic that I occasionally use, and which you'll find quite effective. Let's say that you're very familiar with an item and its value. Let's assume it's worth a hundred dollars to you, and the bidding starts at twenty. The bidding is progressing normally: twenty-five, thirty, thirty-five. Suddenly you jump in and in a loud voice announce, "Sixty dollars!"

This will immediately eliminate and, incidentally, infuriate most of the other buyers. If some brave soul sticks with you, and the bidding starts again at sixty-five, shout, "Eighty!" At this point, the crowd will assume that you're determined to buy this thing at any price, and will allow you, with your obviously immense wealth, to take the item at 80 percent of its value.

I don't recommend using this method too often. People might catch on to what you're doing. Used selectively, however, it will yield good results. The use of this shock bidding will benefit you in another way: You'll begin developing a reputation for aggressive buying. This will intimidate some of the other bidders. You see, people who frequent auctions on a regular basis study the crowd and learn to avoid bidding against certain others.

First, mistaking a movement for a bid doesn't happen that often. The auctioneer, from his vantage point, usually has a pretty good idea of who is actually bidding. A skilled auctioneer can discern the difference between the subtle nod of a bidder and your stretching your neck muscles. Second, if he does mistake an action for a bid, it's no big problem. Simply explain that you weren't bidding. You won't be forced to buy something you don't want.

More often, and more troubling, your bid will be missed. You've raised your eyebrows, pulled your ear lobes, and wrinkled your nose, but somehow your bid was overlooked. The piece is sold to someone else, even though you were willing to up the bid. You've got two choices when this happens. You can either let it go, which is probably best, or you can call the auctioneer's attention to the oversight. When you do this, he will either apologize or, in some rare instances, reopen the bidding. Personally, I feel that once an item is announced, "Sold!" the sale ought to stand. Here again, though, each sale is conducted by an individual, and you're playing by that individual's rules. If you don't like the way the sale is run, you'll just have to go elsewhere.

How to Make Sure Your Bid Is Noticed

At least for your first bid, raise the numbered card you were given when you registered, and shout something like, "Here!" Keep waving it until the auctioneer or one of his helpers acknowledges your offer. Usually this will simply be through eye contact. Once you're recognized as being in the bidding, it's unlikely that you'll go unnoticed during the sale of that lot. In fact, since a surprising number of attendants don't bid at all, once you've been identified as a potential buyer, you'll probably be watched more carefully throughout the auction.

I Bought How Many?

I don't know how many times I've seen bidders shocked when they learn that they have purchased several items when they thought they were buying only one, or to discover that the price they expected to pay has been multiplied a number of times. Sometimes this is discovered at the settlement after the auction ends, in which case the buyer will normally be expected to honor the deal, even though it means spending a lot more than anticipated.

What happens is this: A *group* of similar items is put up for bid, and the auctioneer says something like, "So much apiece and six times the money." This means that the grouping is being sold as a "lot," but the bidding will be based on *per object*. So if six chairs are being sold and the winning bid is $20, for instance, the final price will be six times twenty, or $120.

If several objects are displayed and "choice of the lot" is announced, you're only buying one of the items. The high bidder has the choice of taking as few as one or as many as the entire lot for that bid times the number of items. If only part of the lot is sold, the process is repeated. If there is any misunderstanding during this kind of bidding, it's straightened out at the time, eliminating an unpleasant surprise when it's time to write the check.

You've got to pay close attention when multiple items are on the block. Even when a grouping is started off as "so much apiece," it can be changed in midstream to "choice" or sold as a unit or "lot" for one figure if the auctioneer senses that the first offering isn't going over too well. His job is to get the best price possible while keeping things moving along at a steady pace. Although you might cringe at seeing a set of something broken up, whatever expedient that accomplishes the quick dispersal of the merchandise at the highest price is the one a competent auctioneer will use. Come to think of it, that's the same philosophy successful dealers subscribe to.

It's Worth Exactly What Someone Is Willing to Pay

While any good auctioneer is amazingly knowledgeable about values, you should not allow yourself to be influenced by what they say an item is worth. Decide what value it has for *you*, and stick with it. Any decent auctioneer can always extract another dollar or two from the crowd if he really tries. Any number of tactics might be used.

Auctioneer Arm Twisting

Auctioneers have a number of methods of wheedling a little more money from a reluctant crowd. Among them:

- **Shaming.** "I cannot believe you people don't know what this thing's worth! I thought you were professionals."
- **Prodding.** "I sold one just like this last year for a thousand dollars. You'll look a long time before you find another one of these at any price."
- **Flattery.** "I know you know what this is worth. You think I don't know, don't you?"
- **Cajolery.** "Come on, help me out here. Mrs. Smith had this in her house for eighty years. The family hates to see it go, but frankly, folks, they need the money to settle up this estate."
- **Feigned anger.** "I can't sell it for this price! I'm not gonna do it! It's worth twice that money! I'll buy it myself before I give it away."

Bid Increments

One more word of advice about how the bidding can be controlled. An auctioneer will get into a rhythm while selling a piece and call for bids in certain increments. He might be upping the bids by, let's say, ten dollars at a whack: eighty dollars, ninety dollars, one hundred dollars. When the bidding slows a bit, it's perfectly acceptable for you to inter-ject a bid only five, not ten, dollars more than the last bid. This turns a little of the control over to you.

I suggest that you only do this when the increments are no less than five dollars, though. The auctioneer, and the crowd, become very annoyed with the bidder who slows a sale with twenty-five- and fifty-cent offers. The auctioneer can even refuse to accept such bids.

There Are No Friends at an Auction

If you go to a sale with a friend, are you going to bid against each other when you both want the same thing? Which of you will be polite and let the other get all the bargains? This can be an awkward situation. If it's just a onetime thing and a friend or acquaintance wants to tag along, you'll probably want to show your generosity by allowing your compan-ion first choice. On the other hand, if it's going to be a recurring experi-ence, then you had better make some agreement up front.

When I'm going to find myself in this situation, I try to preview the sale with the other person so that we can discuss our proposed purchases before the bidding begins. We're usually able to agree not to bid against each other on certain items. If we both want something, we know we'll be competing for it, and there will be no hard feelings afterward.

What's This Extra 10 Percent Charge?

Here's another common practice that you should be alerted to: the *buyer's premium*, which is usually an extra 10 percent surcharge added to whatever your purchases total. This charge is always advertised and more commonly occurs at consignment sales. It's a gimmick auction houses use to attract more consignors. Instead of charging them a 15 or 20 percent commission, they might charge only 5 or 10, extracting the rest from you in the form of the buyer's premium.

BIDDING AGAINST A FRIEND

The most commonly used approach to competing on a bid for the same item that a friend is bidding on is looking sur-prised and saying, "Oh! I didn't know you wanted that." Remember, you need your buddy to help you load the truck.

There's nothing wrong with this practice as long as you're aware of it and mentally add the premium to your bids. In my experience, I feel that I end up paying a little more at these sales. But, given the differences in selling prices day to day and the great diversity of merchandise, it's really difficult to make this type of comparison. Once again, just read the advertisement for the sale carefully so you won't be caught unaware at pay-up time.

A Perfect Day for an Auction

There seems to be a common agreement that the worse the weather conditions, the smaller the crowd and, consequently, the better the bargains. I have stood shivering in a chilling drizzle, along with many other miserable bidders, contemplating this myth. The only generalization I can make about weather and auctions is this: If they can hold the sale, people will come to it. Besides, a small crowd doesn't necessarily mean lower prices. What's left when the crowd has dwindled is very often the hard core of buyers. They're there to do business.

A couple of years ago, my wife, knowing that I'm one of the diehards, bought me one of those rain suits. This wonderful garment is simply a raincoat with a hood and a matching pair of waterproof pants. I carry it in the truck all the time. If I'm caught by a sudden storm or attend a sale on one of those rainy days, I find that I'm one of the few people there who's dry.

THE BAG MAN

One resourceful young man I know carries a box of large, plastic trash bags with him to sales. If it begins to rain, he cuts a hole in the bottom for his head and a couple for his arms. They make great emergency ponchos. He also sticks a few in his pocket, so that when others ask him where he got the bag, he can sell them one for a dollar.

Before I got my rain suit, I actually bought one of his bags. You know, standing in the rain among a group of people dressed in garbage bags could make you question the sanity of this business.

The Migration of the Smalls

I'm always amused by the furtive movement of small items from one box lot to another. You might try this sometime: Locate a small, interesting object that's in a box along with a lot of junk.

After you've located such an object, stick it back down in the box, covering it up. Now step back and watch the box. As people paw through the junk and come across the small, precious object, they often will do one of two things: After glancing around to see if anyone is watching, they will shove the thing deep into the bottom, sometimes marking the box for easy recognition later on; or, they'll examine it casually and "accidentally" place it in another box, also covering it carefully. The intent of all this stealthy shuffling is, of course, to have it end up in a box that only one buyer is aware of.

Because of this tendency for smalls to "migrate" from one container to another, you should never assume that a box that you have previously chosen to bid on contains everything it did when you first examined it. Not long ago, I watched a beautifully illustrated, Victorian children's book move through five different boxes.

Despite all this, box lots can be a good source of small collectibles. Sifting through them before or after the purchase is one of the more fun aspects of the game. In one lot that I paid two dollars for recently, I found two sterling silver pickle forks, a silver candle holder, a sterling napkin ring, and a collectible 1898 can opener. I threw out and gave away about thirty pounds of miscellaneous trash that was also in the box, though. They say you've got to kiss a lot of frogs to find a prince, so stay puckered.

Heaven

If you are now or someday become hooked on auctions, you'll probably agree with my idea of Heaven: a warm day in early fall, a big old farmhouse, way out in the country, that has been in the family for a hundred years; the smells of musty upholstery and sun-warmed, old wood mingling with the aroma of hot dogs, burning leaves, and apples that have fallen to the ground.

The ladies' auxiliary is offering homemade pie, strong coffee, and country-ham sandwiches. The crowd is of moderate size and most are just looking. And there's so much to choose from, and things are going so cheaply, that you have to restrain yourself from buying too much. While this might sound like a fantasy or a dream, we all happen on these sales now and again.

▸2◂

other sources of merchandise

In financial and real estate circles, the term OPM means "Other People's Money." For instance, a piece of property might be mortgaged to buy another piece of property, and then the new property pays for itself through rents or whatever. In other words, no cash has been laid out by the buyer; hence, other people's money is being used to purchase the second property.

In the antiques business you can't operate like this. But I like to refer to sources other than auctions for buying antiques as "Other People's Merchandise." We'll apply this term only to things purchased from people who are intent on selling that or some related item, however. See chapter 5 for merchandise you can acquire for nothing, or from unexpected sources.

Antiques Shops

The first and most obvious sources for antiques for resale are antiques shops and multiple-dealer antiques centers. Don't scoff. Every dealer does it. Invariably, if you visit enough shops, you'll find things that are underpriced: things that still have some margin for a profit to be made. You can usually purchase these things at a further discount because you are a dealer.

The pickings are much better at large antiques centers, or malls, of course. The nature of these centers makes them ideal for novice dealers. Wherever you have dealers just entering the business, you will find some bargains. Naturally, these new dealers might also price some things too high. You just have to use good judgment. Don't assume everything is underpriced just because a few items are. The very best time to get bargains is when a new antiques mall first opens: Then it's just chock-full of fledgling dealers.

Go ahead and take advantage of their inexperience. Someone sure will. Provide them with a valuable learning experience. When they see their merchandise in your shop at a healthy markup, they will be wiser.

I remember when I first set up a real shop. I had been fooling around with antiques for years but had no real experience in pricing a general line of merchandise. At the end of a couple of weeks I had sold a lot more than I had expected to sell, but about 80 percent of my sales were to other dealers. I recognized my merchandise in other people's shops for months after that.

But you know what? That didn't bother me a bit. I made a profit and that's the name of the game. To this day I try to keep my prices low enough to sell to both dealers and individuals. Why should I care that someone will make a profit from something they bought from me? In most cases my profit is at least 100 percent — and very often 1,000 percent. That dealer who buys from me is probably only going to make 20 or 30 percent. We both make money, though. We're both happy.

THE TRAVELING TABLE

You can't let it bother you when someone buys your merchandise, moves it around the corner, and puts a big price on it. Once, I purchased a nice little mahogany table — more a candle stand — for sixty dollars. It was unusual because it had drop leaves. I refinished it and took it to the antiques center where I was renting a space. There I priced it at eighty dollars. Not a big profit for my work, but I didn't feel it was worth any more. It sold before I left the shop.

When my wife and I left the center, we decided to have lunch at a small town nearby that is famous for its many small, exclusive antiques shops. As we were strolling down the street, we happened to spot the owner of one of the shops taking "our" table into his store. Later, we dropped by out of curiosity and noted that the little stand was now priced at $125.

"It'll never sell at that price," we chuckled to ourselves. Two weeks later I found my table in another antiques center for $150. Could I have sold it originally for that? Maybe. Probably. Who knows?

Take the Money and Run

There are three points I want to make about buying and selling among dealers:

1. If you make a profit, take it and forget it. Don't worry about what someone else is making off you. Does the cattle rancher concern himself with the price of a hamburger at one of the big chains? Does he try to calculate how many burgers they got out of one of his cows?
2. I truly believe that more than half of all antiques go through several dealers' hands before ending up in someone's home. Sometimes I think that if it weren't for the trade among dealers, there would be next to no trade at all.
3. I keep repeating this, I know, but it's true that there is no right price for most antiques. If it's unique or rare, it's worth what someone is willing to pay. Even things that seem to have established "book" prices can fluctuate drastically.

Mining the Classified Ads

Another source I've had pretty good luck with is classified advertising in the newspapers. I get newspapers from several surrounding towns and peruse the ads almost daily. Although I look at the antiques category in the ads, I rarely find anything of interest. Usually those ads are placed by dealers, or if not, by someone who wants to get top price for a family heirloom. Don't forget that you only buy at wholesale.

The ads that yield the best results for me are under "Furniture" and "Miscellaneous." I try to scan these ads fairly thoroughly, but that doesn't mean I read every word. What I'm looking for are *key* words. Words that cause me to pause include: OLD, OAK, MAHOGANY, MARBLE, BRASS, or UNUSUAL. You get the idea.

Buried in that ad for baby clothes, a beanbag chair, and an upright freezer, will occasionally be the "fancy, old table" or "oak rocking chair," or some other telling phrase. The people who placed these ads aren't selling antiques. They're just getting rid of surplus and unwanted items. Of course, that fancy old table might turn out to be a twenty-year-old relic from a discount store, but now and then you hit pay dirt. I call this "mining the ads" because you've got to dig through so much extraneous information to find those nuggets that turn out to be genuine antiques.

Identify Yourself

When you check out the item and it's something you want, the first thing to do is ask the price. The next thing, regardless of whether you

---

TWO TIPS

Here are two tips that will save you money when buying from individuals:

1. When you ask to see anything else they might want to sell, phrase your request as a desire to see anything old, not antique. The term *antique* implies "value" to most people, while the term *old* connotes "used." And don't ask if they want to sell it; ask if they want to get rid of it. These are subtle differences in terminology, to be sure, but they can change the way a person perceives an object.

2. When you're ready to make an offer, bring a roll of dollar bills from your pocket, and phrase your offer like this: "Would you take a hundred dollars for it right now?" There's something about the sight of cash and the prospect of getting it right now, that works wonders. You might have enough in your checking account to buy everything in the house, but that check just doesn't have the same impact as a hundred dollar bill.

---

intend to make an offer or not, is to present a card and let them know that you're a dealer. A lot of new dealers are reluctant to do this. They figure that this will alert the seller to the possibility that the item might be worth more than they thought. They fear that the item might be withdrawn or the seller might try to negotiate a higher price.

I haven't found that to be the case. If you explain that you can't afford to pay a lot because you have expenses and overhead, you might be surprised to find that you can get a better price. Often people are just happy to be able to get rid of some old thing that doesn't go with their modern furnishings.

Besides, if you don't tell them up front that you're a dealer, how are you going to ask them the next question: "Do you have anything else old that you want to get rid of?" It's surprising what people have in their basements, attics, and garages, and what little value they sometimes place on them. You see, there are two types of people out there: people like you and me, who love antiques, and those who don't.

Flea Markets

Forgive me if you are a fan of flea markets, but now I cringe when I see the word. There was a time when flea markets were fun places to visit, and genuine collectibles and antiques dominated the available merchandise. Now I go to a large flea market and feel that I'm at a carnival without the rides. The sellers of cheap, gaudy, inferior new merchandise seem to outnumber those dealing in antiques ten to one.

This might not be true in your area, and admittedly, it isn't true of every flea market I visit, but it seems more and more to be the rule rather than the exception. They're okay if you're in the market for a bundle of tube socks or a lamp that sprouts glass fibers that light up. Guess what, though. I still go to flea markets. I go to them because I'm a capitalist, intent on making a profit, and there are still some bargains to be had there.

Exercise caution, though, if you shop at these places. Flea markets abound with reproductions. Unless you're skillful at detection, you should be very cautious when buying such things as Depression glass, pottery, or cast-iron items. If you discover that you've bought a fake, the dealer might not be there when you go back to complain.

Buy only what you're familiar with. Don't be tempted by what appears to be a bargain. Be a shrewd buyer like me. By the way, do you need any socks? I've got this huge bundle of tube socks I bought the other day . . .

Whoa! Pull Over!

My wife tells me that we need to get a bumper sticker that says, "I brake for every yard sale." Well, I don't, but I don't miss many. The yard sale, or tag sale, has become an American institution. It combines the attributes of a flea market, an auction, and the classifieds.

This is such an obvious source of OPM that it barely warrants mentioning. But for the uninitiated, you could be overlooking an opportunity to find some surprising bargains. Remember, rock-bottom prices are the lure of yard sales. The people holding them are generally clearing out things they have accumulated and no longer want. They don't want to carry it all back into the house.

Almost every yard sale I stop at yields something. It might be a fifty-cent piece of Depression glass or a McCoy vase. In fact, yard sales are one of the last remaining places where you can still find underpriced art pottery. I have found Weller, Roseville, and McCoy, along with other less valuable, but still collectible, pieces at these sales. This stuff keeps coming to the surface as people rid themselves of what they consider to be ugly, drab, or just old-fashioned. While a flowerpot from the thirties might not be exactly a treasure, picked up for a few cents or a dollar and sold for many times that, it makes it well worth the few minutes it takes to stop at a yard sale.

Actually, you might not even have to stop at all. I've trained myself to scan the merchandise as I slowly pass by, and I only pull over if I spot something that looks like a possibility. More than once, I have stopped at a sale on my way to the shop and made a purchase that paid for my gas or lunch that day. On a few occasions, the stop has bought our groceries for a week.

Look Beyond the Table

Depending on how busy you are, what the general collection of odds and ends are, how old the house and the owners appear to be, and how much cash you have in your pocket, a yard sale is one more ideal situation where you can get yourself invited in to check out other possible buys. Don't pass up the chance to look beyond what's on the table.

As I suggested you do when responding to a classified ad, you should tell the folks holding a yard sale that you would be interested in seeing anything else old that they might want to rid themselves of. There might be something in the house, barn, or garage that was too heavy to haul up on the front lawn. Use your status as a dealer to be nosy. You'll never know unless you ask. I think I've actually bought more this way than from the items on display.

Pssst! Ya Wanna Buy a Clock?

It's unwise to buy things from people who bring them to you, unless you know the people or can get someone reliable to vouch for them.

In no way should you interpret this to mean that pickers, as a group or individually, are dishonest. They're in the same business you're in. It's just that anyone unknown to you who arrives at your door with something to sell should be regarded with some suspicion. Would you buy a diamond ring from a guy on the street corner?

You don't need to know very much about the person you sell something to, but you should always know who you're buying from.

Placing Classified Ads

Some dealers run ads offering to buy antiques. It can yield results, but for the small or new dealer I'm not sure I'd recommend it. When I experimented with this in the past, I found that I was at a slight disadvantage. People assumed that if I had to advertise, then I must be in dire need of what they had to sell. I was rarely able to negotiate a really good deal.

I'll go into this deeper a little further on, but if you place ads offering to buy, be sure you go to the seller. It's not a good idea to buy from strangers who bring things to you. If you do, you risk being a receiver of stolen goods. Just be careful who you deal with in a situation like this. It's especially risky if you're advertising for a specific item. This seems to create a ready market for someone to "steal to order" the thing you want.

Pick Your Picker Prudently

Unless you have a good-sized shop and sell antiques full time, you might never deal with *pickers*. You should know about them, though, since, at the very least, they will be your competitors at auctions.

Pickers are individuals who buy antiques at auction or elsewhere for the sole purpose of reselling them to dealers. Many dealers who have shops to run cannot or don't wish to take the time to attend auctions; they rely almost solely on pickers as their suppliers of antiques.

A picker's profit margin won't be nearly as large as yours, but he generally has little or no overhead, except for the truck he uses to haul the merchandise. Some dealers have standing orders with certain pickers for particular types of merchandise. Other pickers buy whatever they're pretty sure they can sell, and travel to several shops with their purchases. They are, in effect, acting as agents for the dealers and collect a commission on what they sell.

Some pickers buy so much and are such consistent customers that they become cozy with a number of auctioneers. Whether it's intentional or not, it sometimes appears that they receive preferential treatment from them. It can be a little annoying, but you shouldn't be intimidated by or hesitate to bid against them.

In fact, even if you don't ever expect to buy truckloads of merchandise from them, it's not a bad idea to cultivate a relationship with a few of these folks. Since they generally have a network of buyers looking for particular types of merchandise, you might ask one of them to act as a middleman for selling something you can't seem to get rid of. Sometimes a quick sale, even if it's at your cost, is preferable to having something take up space in a shop for too long.

Sit and Wait for It

This sort of goes along with buying from pickers, and certainly all the warnings about not buying from total strangers should be heeded. But if you're known to be actively seeking certain categories of antiques or collectibles, people will seek you out and offer you deals. People know I can't resist pottery or lamps, so they constantly bring these items to me.

Since I also repair those items, I'm in an especially good position to see a lot of what dealers are planning to sell. If I can make them a reasonable offer, before they spend the money to have it fixed, we both get what we want. They make some profit, and I get it *cheap!* (In chapter 5, you'll read a lot more about the advantages of developing these sidelines.)

Other people's merchandise: It's everywhere you care to look. It's in basements, garages, and barns; it's in other dealers' shops and on the backs of pickers' trucks. You spot it on the front porch of a bungalow in town and behind the counter at a diner where you stop on the way to a sale. Maybe it's for sale. Maybe you can get it cheap.

▸3◂

what you
shouldn't buy

A lot of new dealers make the same mistake: They do a lot of indiscriminate buying in an attempt to quickly stock their first shop. Then through trial and error, they weed out all the types of merchandise that don't sell. By that time, unfortunately, many of them have become discouraged by what they think is a completely "hit-or-miss" business, and they simply quit. If they don't quit out of discouragement, there's a good chance their funds will run out and they'll be forced to give up.

In this chapter, I show you how to avoid some of the more common pitfalls and teach you a good basic buying strategy. Perhaps with some guidance, you won't become disenchanted with what can be a fun and profitable business.

Suggesting the types of things that you should and shouldn't buy is a little risky, since regional tastes have so much influence on the antiques trade. In addition, since fads and decorating trends have such an impact on the public's buying patterns, there's a danger of telling you something now that won't be true next year.

In fact, several people have suggested that it's pretty arrogant of me to try and tell you what to buy, so I won't do that. Well, I won't do that in this chapter. In this chapter, I'll just tell you what to avoid. In chapter 4, presumptuous or not, I *will* tell you what to buy.

While it's certainly impossible for me to give you guaranteed, hard-and-fast rules for every situation, I think that by adhering to the do's and don'ts provided in this and the next chapter, you'll be better equipped to weather the early stages of going into the antiques business. Traditionally, it's the *learning* stage that kills off so many of us in this trade.

Don't Be Unduly Influenced by Fads and Trends

It might not be as obvious as it is in, say, the clothing industry, but fads and trends definitely affect what people buy from antiques and collectibles dealers. Consequently, they will have at least an indirect effect on what you acquire for resale. The trick is in not allowing too many of your buying decisions to be based on brief infatuations.

First, let's examine the differences between the terms *fad* and *trend* as they apply to you, the antiques dealer. Fads seem to pop up out of nowhere and die just as quickly. Trends, on the other hand, creep up on us gradually and just sort of fade away without making much fuss. You have to learn to distinguish between the two and act accordingly.

Common Fads

Here's an example of a common fad in our business: A popular magazine runs an article on collecting vintage rolling pins. You can bet there will be a run on these things. Suddenly, you sell the two or three that have been gathering dust in your shop. You might be tempted to buy all you can get your hands on because, not only did you sell yours, customers are actually asking for them. One month later, the next issue comes out and everyone wants green-handled, Depression-era kitchen utensils.

IF ANDY HAD 'EM, I WANT 'EM

Probably the most famous example of a fad that had far-reaching effects was the 1988 auction of artist Andy Warhol's collection of McCoy cookie jars. They sold for astronomical prices that had absolutely nothing to do with their value. If I, many other dealers, and collectors had been able to unload our cookie jars for such ridiculous money, we'd all be sitting on the beach somewhere in the tropics.

While the overall value of cookie jars did not increase to anywhere near the proportions realized at that auction, the publicity the sale received did serve to focus more interest on something that was already being collected by many people. This, in itself, drove prices up. A few people even got caught up in the frenzy and paid far more than they're ever likely to get for them.

How do you adjust your buying to accommodate these sudden surges of interest? My advice to you: Don't even try! There will be opportunities to take advantage of the situation, but trying to keep up with this type of demand will only drive you crazy and get you in trouble.

Trends

How do trends operate, and what do you need to know to buy intelligently so that your inventory somewhat reflects them? First of all, you need to know that there is usually more than one trend operating at any given time.

Trends, you'll discover, are at least in part generational, meaning that people in different age groups tend to want to own things from different eras. For instance, "baby boomers" now make up a huge portion of the buying public. They seem to be searching, in large part, for things that remind them of their youth or childhood. If you, as a dealer, are of this generation, then you already have a good idea what part of your inventory should consist of.

The thing is, if you are in this age group, you might be overlooking a lucrative market in collectibles that appeals to a younger crowd. A lot of this material is not going to strike you as attractive or even tasteful. Not only that, you might not even be aware of what evokes feelings of nostalgia in this group.

Is it really all that complicated? Not in the least. It just means that if you're young, you're going to have to talk to us "older" folks and vice versa. It's the only way to get a feel for what people of varying ages like.

The trick in this case is balance. If you take all the preceding factors into consideration, you can begin to establish an inventory representative of most tastes. Now, let's get a little more specific about what you should avoid.

WHAT ABOUT *TRUE* ANTIQUES?

In all this talk about collectibles, fads, and trends, it's easy to lose sight of the fact that there is always a market for items that have intrinsic value, that are classic and timeless. True antiques (technically those things that exceed one hundred years of age), precede all the age groups and will always be sought by collectors and decorators.

Don't Buy What You Like

A number of you will disagree with me here because you've spent the last few years building a big collection of decorated stoneware or Wallace Nutting prints. Maybe you've accumulated a thousand pairs of salt-and-pepper shakers or shelves full of miniature oil lamps. Now you want to turn your hobby into a profitable business venture. Let's see, I've got three hundred of these whatchamacallits, and they're worth a hundred dollars apiece. When I've accumulated about a hundred more, I'll open a shop and sit back while the money rolls in.

I strongly suggest that you continue to enjoy your hobby but that you don't waste a lot of time or money on trying to develop it into a viable retail business. I've seen dealer after dealer try this and fail. They think, "Gee, as a collector I would have loved finding a shop like this!" The thing is, how many more of you are out there? More importantly, how many of them are going to just happen onto your shop?

If you've got a really huge collection and can become known as the source for this merchandise, and if you're willing to advertise outside your area, you might possibly attract enough business to make your efforts worthwhile. That's assuming that what you're selling lends itself to mail-order merchandising.

I know, I know. This takes a lot of the fun out of it for some would-be dealers. But if your goal is to actually realize a profit, you're going to have to cater to as broad a cross section of the population as possible. I insist that this business has to be fun, and it's no fun when you spend a lot of time worrying about making enough money to pay the rent.

OKAY, I'LL RELENT — JUST A LITTLE

You must buy with the general public in mind, but that doesn't mean you can't specialize in one thing or the other (preferably, at least two unrelated things). It's fine, as long as you also provide for a more eclectic or diverse stock at the same time.

Since you like antiques, you're bound to like some period or category better than others. And you probably know more about that period or category than you do most other things. Use that knowledge and love to your advantage in becoming the expert in that field, but don't neglect the larger problem of keeping the money coming in.

Don't Buy What Every Other Dealer Is Selling

As you walk among the stalls of the average antiques mall, you'll see certain items that every dealer seems to have. You might assume from this that these items sell well. Otherwise why would so many dealers be offering them? Maybe it's because some things just seem to belong in every shop, and, well, since everybody else is selling them . . .

Let's look at an example: oak washstands. Up through the early part of the twentieth century, they were about the most common piece of furniture in existence. Where a home would have had only one buffet or sideboard, it most likely held several washstands, one in each bedroom.

Don't get me wrong — washstands do sell. In fact, they're very popular. The problem is that — and this applies to any item that's fairly plentiful — unless the one you're planning to sell is in some way unique, the chances of its selling are reduced to luck, that is, unless you can sell yours cheaper. Therefore, if you can't buy it at a price that will allow you to undersell everyone else, it's best to avoid the purchase. We'll look closer at pricing in chapter 19, but for now it's enough to understand that uniqueness is an important factor in this business.

You absolutely must, especially in the beginning, have turnover foremost in your mind when stocking your shop. It's the basis of your survival. And the smaller your inventory, the faster you must turn it over (for a profit). Simply put, you can't afford to have something taking up valuable space just because it's pretty.

No matter how you strive to keep the stock in your shop different from all the others, the luck factor will always account for a good percentage of your sales. Nevertheless, consistency in sales will make the difference between success and failure.

So before you go out and buy your first truckload of merchandise to fill your shop, you'd be well advised to do a little market research. Time invested in scouting out existing dealers is time well spent.

Don't Take the Risk
Unless the Risk Is Worth Taking

There are two classifications of antiques or collectibles that you should consider very carefully before buying: items that have been extensively reproduced and familiar but unmarked pieces.

Reproductions

Unfortunately, many collectibles are being reproduced. Among them are:

▸ Certain Depression-glass patterns and pieces
▸ Vintage movie posters
▸ Prints and advertising art
▸ Toys (especially tin, wind-up)
▸ Mechanical and still banks
▸ Art pottery
▸ Tiffany-style lamps
▸ Doorstops and other cast-iron items

Moreover, there are always a number of unscrupulous dealers at work putting "repro" prints in old frames, "aging" those cast-iron items on the back lawn, and making the new toys look as if they've been abused by several generations of children. Add in the honest dealers who are unknowingly presenting these items for sale as authentic because they themselves were duped, and you can see what you're up against.

Naturally, you don't want to buy these reproductions for resale in your shop. That's a good way to damage your reputation, something that you'll find is one of your greatest assets. But just as importantly, you're going to have to avoid buying items that are not fakes themselves but that are being duplicated. When, for instance, people see a lot of cobalt-blue Shirley Temple cream pitchers everywhere they turn, they soon get the idea that many of them have to be reproductions. So even if the one you're selling is authentic, your prospective customers are going to be leery of buying it. In this way, a good collectible becomes devalued and more difficult to sell. Ironically, if the piece is "mint," it becomes even more suspect because of its pristine condition.

Unfortunately, I can't teach you how to recognize such fakes in this book. Mostly it's time and experience that give you that ability, but even then the most cautious of dealers, including me, still gets burned now and again. By paying close attention as you peruse the shops, you'll begin noticing when an item is a little too plentiful.

It's usually only the highly desirable, expensive objects that interest those who make reproductions, though. For the same reason that counterfeiters don't print one dollar bills, the people who reproduce collectibles and who fake antiques don't bother with the "low-ticket" items.

Every part of the country has periodicals dealing with antiques. Such regional publications as *Antique Week* and such nationally distributed papers as *Warman's Today's Collector* often warn readers of the arrival of reproductions on the antiques scene. I advise you to read them, not only because they run articles on fake collectibles but also because they're such good sources of general knowledge about the business. And the more you know about a subject the less likely you are to be fooled. (See Suggested Reading and References at the back of this book for other ideas.)

A lot of price and identification guides also alert readers to known counterfeits. Sometimes they're very specific, warning collectors to be on the lookout for a particular item and describing the differences between the real item and the faked one. If for no other reason than that, I would strongly recommend that you begin to accumulate a good library of these books. Even though the values quoted quickly become outdated, they're still excellent references and contain a wealth of educational material.

ADVERTISED REPRODUCTIONS

If you look at the newspapers and other publications written for the antiques and collectibles trade, you'll see ads placed by companies that specialize in selling reproductions to dealers. If they have a catalog, order it. Not because I want you to sell reproductions in your shop, but because it will give you one more good source of information about what is being reproduced.

In defense of the companies that sell these goods, they are not misrepresenting their merchandise. They are selling *reproductions*, and they make that clear. It's in the *aftermarket* (i.e., the resale market) that the distinction gets lost.

THE CHEAP REFERENCE LIBRARY

As an author who gets paid when a book sells, I should probably be shot for the advice I'm going to give you now. But as The World's Cheapest Antiques Dealer, I just can't pass up a chance to save you some more money.

You know that I advocate owning as large a reference library as possible (I also advocate toting a good portion of those books around with you when you shop, by the way), but because updating your library can be prohibitively expensive, you need to find a way to lessen that expense (remember that expenses are deductible at tax time, though). Try this:

1. Get your friends together and order in quantity. You can often get a discount of up to 40 percent when you buy a number of books from the publisher.

2. Make an arrangement with a couple of other dealers to update part of a mutually owned library each year. In other words, I'll buy a couple this year, and you buy a couple next year. It's not like having your own at your fingertips when you need it, though.

3. Here's where I get shot. If you have a used bookstore nearby, chances are you've struck gold. Since many dealers replace their books often, there's usually a number of P-and-I's on the shelf at greatly reduced prices. As I said, the values will be outdated, but by looking back over several years of publication, you can usually estimate the rate, or percentage, at which a collectible is appreciating. Don't depend too heavily on this system, though, as prices can take some pretty drastic leaps from year to year.

Price-and-Identification Books

Let's digress just a bit, to discuss price-and-identification (P-and-I) guidebooks. There are literally hundreds of them published. Collector Books of Paducah, Kentucky, for example, offers more than two hundred such books, and for the most part they're updated, at least for values, every year. This means that if you use them as price guides, you're going to have to replace your books often. With few exceptions, I don't do that.

The best reason for owning them is that they allow you to begin to recognize collectibles that you would otherwise overlook. You'll do well to spend some of your time just leafing through these publications. You'll be surprised at how much you retain. On many occasions I've picked up bargains on things that no one else spotted, because I had just seen the item in one of my many P-and-I guides.

Should You Buy It?

What should an inexperienced dealer or collector do, then, when faced with an opportunity to buy something that appears authentic but is somewhat questionable or even something that's known to be real but also known to be often reproduced? Until you feel really comfortable assessing the authenticity of an item, this is a a risk that's not worth taking. Pass it up. You've got an unlimited supply of less risky material out there to spend your money on.

Familiar but Unmarked Items

Another closely related category of collectibles that you must be wary of is the *familiar* item: the one that looks like others you've seen but isn't signed (in the antiques trade, "signed" doesn't mean with a signature in most cases, but rather an imprint or some other identifying mark). For example, you see something that you're positive should be marked Weller or Pairpont or Nutting, but no matter how closely you look, you can't find a mark.

Here, I was going to say something like, "Better safe than sorry." Then, I started thinking about the rare pieces of pottery, unsigned but still worth hundreds of dollars, that I've bought for a tiny fraction of their value, and I remember the Stangl bird that my wife discovered recently. It was mounted on a homemade lamp, so that the inscription on the base was hidden. We recognize these "hidden" treasures only because we're well acquainted with the characteristics of these particular items. There are, however, many purchases we pass up because we're not so familiar with them.

I realize I'm cautioning and enticing you at the same time. One of the primary reasons I'm in this business is the joy of discovery — the thrill of finding something valuable that others overlook or are afraid to take a chance on. So what, you may ask, is my advice? Take the chance? Don't take the chance? Am I once more contradicting my usual, conservative self? No, my advice that you take the chance if the chance is worth taking, still stands.

The key word, of course, is *if*. But, how does that work? How do you decide if making a purchase of an unmarked collectible is wise or not?

Let me use an example. I see an object that I'm confident is worth two hundred dollars. It's not marked, but I'm pretty sure I saw it in one of my books. It's priced at one hundred dollars. Wow! If I'm right, I can double my money. Sorry, I'll pass on this one but if I can get it for twenty bucks, then I'll take the risk.

The whole point to gambling is risking small amounts of money in the hope of a big payoff, a return much larger than the original "investment." Otherwise, why bother? If racetracks promised to return only your original bet when your horse won, who would bother to wager? Casinos wouldn't stay in business very long if they had big, flashy signs advertising, "Jackpot — Get Your Quarter Back!"

Maybe I've overemphasized my point, but unless you set some strict limits on what you're willing to risk and refuse to gamble on a purchase unless you can expect a large return on it, you'll find yourself just breaking even all the time. While you might think shooting for a 900 percent profit seems excessive or even greedy, you'll be wrong often enough to make this policy justifiable. Just getting your money back on too many purchases won't keep you in business.

Let's look at a few more categories that you'd be wise to avoid.

Don't Buy China or Glassware That's Chipped or Cracked

Auctioneers and some dealers just love to toss around the term *usage marks* when referring to damaged glassware. I guess this sounds a lot better than asking, "What will you give for this broken vase?"

Seriously now, would you buy a wrecked car from a dealer because he tells you, "Oh, these might look like dents, but they're just usage marks?" You probably wouldn't, but many succumb to this tactic when it's used to describe a less-than-perfect vinegar cruet.

Of course it's used! It's an antique! But it's also broken, folks. There's enough of the good stuff available without resorting to buying defective merchandise. Your customers, for the most part, will pass these things up.

Don't Buy Coins or Stamps

Unless you're an expert, coins are a very risky business. There's a huge difference, in the eyes of a collector, between a coin in mint condition and one in very fine condition. Naturally, it follows that there's a big difference in value, too.

Aside from that, coin collectors aren't like other collectors; they don't usually frequent antiques shops in search of additions to their collections. The fact that coin and stamp dealers don't usually survive in antiques malls when surrounded by other types of antiques dealers has a lot to do with specialization, which I don't recommend.

Don't Buy Painted Furniture

Unless you're a glutton for punishment and have a lot of time on your hands, you should probably forgo the purchase of most painted furniture — that is, unless you intend to either sell it as is or repaint it.

It's so easy to imagine that lavender dresser or that "antiqued" parlor table with its natural wood uncovered and its lovely grain glowing warmly. Believe me when I tell you that you don't know what's under that paint. There might be filled gouges, missing veneer, or mismatched woods. Much old furniture, especially lower-quality Victorian pieces, contain several types of wood with dissimilar grain patterns and characteristics. It was common practice by the manufacturers to mix these materials, since the furniture was stained very dark and often coated with pigmented finishes.

When you strip and attempt to stain these pieces, you'll find it nearly impossible to get an acceptably even coloring over the entire object. Unfortunately, the stuff that tends to be easier to strip (like oak, which I'll cover later) brings nearly as high a price painted as it does in its natural state. Why put yourself through all that work and aggravation?

Enough with the Don'ts

Well, I suppose that's about enough of this negative stuff. I've learned that most people (like my daughters when they were youngsters) get tired of hearing me say "don't" all the time. Although my intentions are good — I just want you to learn from my mistakes — it's generally more fun to hear about what works than about what doesn't. Come to think of it, my kids weren't all that crazy about being told what *to* do, either.

Regardless, in the next chapter we'll move on to a discussion of what I feel will enable a beginning dealer to purchase, wisely, a good starting inventory.

LOOKING BEYOND THE OBVIOUS

Did I tell you not to buy stamps? Okay, now let me tell you about a really good deal I got on some stamps at an estate sale. The ad for the sale mentioned that several stamp albums were being offered. Because of this, a number of collectors were on hand in search of bargains.

I watched as they leafed through the albums and poked around in a small box of loose stamps. I'm not a philatelist myself, but being eternally curious, I just had to nose around a bit. The box, I noticed, was full of current unused stamps, not old, postmarked stamps.

When it came time for the stamps to be sold, the collectors competed vigorously for the albums. When the little box of loose stamps came up, the collectors, every one of them, were totally uninterested. Since only the "stamps people" (and nosy me) had bothered to look in the box in the first place, no one else was aware of its contents. This is no lie, I bought fifty dollars worth of good, usable postage for fifty cents! *All* of our friends got Christmas cards that year!

I don't tell you this story with the expectation that you're going to go to the next auction and find a fistful of postage stamps. I relate it to emphasize how important it is to look beyond the obvious.

▸4◂

what you *should* buy

Most of the books that I've read about buying and selling antiques talk a lot about how to buy but very little about what to buy. So I decided to tell you with this book not only the *what*, but the why. As I said in the last chapter, my suggestions are intended to get you started with an inexpensive, basic inventory.

One reason most books don't discuss what to buy is the differences in regional tastes. Since this book isn't large enough to cover all regional possibilities, this chapter concentrates on those items that sell just about anywhere.

Hopefully, these suggestions will serve you well over time. Even though my interests have varied over the years and I sometimes go off on tangents, I find myself returning to these basics continually in order to generate profits to keep me in the business. Let's plunge right in and take a look at the "do" list.

Do Buy Painted Furniture

Hold on there! Did I fall asleep between chapters and forget that I told you not to buy painted furniture? Not really. Remember, I said don't buy it unless you intend to sell it "as is" or repaint it.

There's generally available a pretty good supply of furniture that was painted by its owners during one of those periods when that practice was fashionable. Perhaps a particular wood lost favor and wasn't considered stylish anymore. There was even a period in the 1960s and early 1970s when "antiquing" in shades of green, red, or blue, streaked with darker "graining," was the craze. Whatever the reason, the fact that it was painted can work to your advantage.

Because of the difficulties encountered in stripping and refinishing painted pieces, many people refuse to buy them. For this reason, sturdy items with nice lines are often sold for a song. I've even had them given to me or picked them out of junk piles after auctions.

For now, let me just say that if you see something that you can envision as lovely with a marble top or exquisite in, maybe, "burled" walnut, and it's dirt cheap, you should buy it. In chapter 7, I'll show you, even if you consider yourself "artistically challenged," how you can apply some simple faux finishing techniques that will transform your purchases and convert them from junk to money!

The Oak Exception

Painted oak furniture that sells for less than it would if it were unpainted is a good candidate for stripping and refinishing. Because of the wood's hardness and the types of finishes that are initially applied by furniture makers, oak will strip nicely about nine times out of ten. In chapter 8, I'll guide you through the stripping process. That job doesn't have to be as hard as most people make it.

Do Buy Damaged Art Pottery

You are paying attention. Yes, I previously warned you about the folly of buying glassware and china with "usage" marks. So why in the world would I recommend that you spend good money on a piece of broken art pottery? And for the uninitiated, what is art pottery, anyway?

Art pottery is a term applied to the decorative ceramics manufactured by such defunct companies as Weller, Hull, McCoy, and Roseville. There are quite a few others, but these names will constitute the bulk of what you see in the collectibles market. I refer to them as the "Big Four." I'm not even going to attempt an explanation beyond that for now. If you're in any way associated with the antiques business, you can't help but come into contact with this category of highly desirable collectibles.

I like art pottery for its aesthetic qualities but also because it retains much of its value, even after repair (if the repair is done well). You can't say that about china or glassware.

I hate to harp on something, but here's another case where I urge you to get some reference books. Those depicting the outputs of at least the Big Four manufacturers are almost essential if you're going to be in the business. This is one area of collectibles where prices increase steadily, and in some cases tremendously, from year to year. It's also one of the few situations where the prices quoted in these various guidebooks are pretty closely adhered to. Quite often, in fact, collectors willingly pay more than "book" value for some lines.

And if there's an exception to my rule of buying used price-and-identification guides when you can, this would be it. Current guides will be more helpful in this case, but remember what I said in chapter 3 (page 36) about estimating the rate of increasing values.

If you're willing to learn a new skill (I contend almost anyone can), in chapter 12 I'll explain how to repair and color the most common types of damage.

Do Buy Old Prints

Vintage lithographs, prints, and photos have always been a mainstay of the antiques business, so my telling you to buy them should come as no big surprise. You could have figured that one out yourself, right? But wait, did you think The World's Cheapest Antiques Dealer would let you off that easy? What I buy, and what I want you to buy, is the bargain that all the others are going to ignore.

This bargain comes in two forms: (1) the absolutely wonderful print in the horrible frame, and (2) the absolutely horrible print in the wonderful frame.

For some reason, bargains like these are overlooked by many dealers. After purchasing a few yourself, you'll see how combining "good" prints with "good" frames can yield a continuous supply of salable art. Though matching art and frame size might seem like a problem at first glance, judicious trimming of pictures that are too large and the addition of oversized mats to those that are too small are relatively quick fixes.

The Incongruous Combination

The idea of matching up pictures and frames is obvious. So let's move on to a concept that's a little more complex. If you see a print that's not very special but seems much newer than the frame it's in, buy it! Look for the following before you buy:

1. The frame should be old. I don't care if it looks like it's been run over by a truck, as long as it's got some age on it.
2. When you examine the back of the picture very carefully, it should be obvious that the backing hasn't been removed recently. You can usually tell this by looking at the nails. Do they have fresh scratches on them? Are some of them newer than the others? Are there any tell-tale marks on the backing that indicate that the nails have been removed and replaced?
3. If the print is something from the 1940s (maybe a calendar print or a photo of FDR) or later, and if the frame is obviously earlier than that, buy it. You might be in luck.
4. Since you're buying a possible disaster, consider price. It's got to be cheap!

If all these conditions are met, there's a fair-to-good chance that your gamble will pay off. You see, many people who grow tired of looking at a picture simply insert a more up-to-date one in its frame, placing it over the existing print.

In my home, I can point out five beautiful prints, their colors still vivid after being preserved behind other pictures for sixty years or more. Two are Currier and Ives originals, two are classic Victorian indoor scenes, and one is a priceless RCA "Nipper" dog advertising piece. I didn't pay more than two dollars for any of them.

What Have You Lost?

If you follow my advice, I guarantee that your efforts will be rewarded. After all, if the frame is shot and the worthless picture that was visible all along turns out to be the only thing in it, what have you really lost? At the very least, you usually have a piece of glass that's worth what you've spent.

By now everyone's heard the story of the guy who found an original of the Declaration of Independence in the back of an old frame. Maybe you can get that lucky. Well, maybe not. But satisfying one's curiosity alone is sometimes worth a couple of bucks.

At Least Take It Apart to Clean It

I'm always puzzled by the dealers who buy prints and never take them apart, even to clean them. Remember, these things hung in houses that were lit by kerosene and heated by wood or coal. Soot and dirt has collected, not only on the outside, but on the inside as well. You'll be amazed at what's accumulated over time, and how much more presentable a print becomes after cleaning (see the accompanying box).

CLEANING PAPER WITH BREAD

Some of the most difficult items to clean are those made of paper. Old prints, documents, and advertising *ephemera* (a fancy word you'll see referring to paper collectibles) become very soiled over time, even when framed and covered with glass.

There is a safe procedure for cleaning: Lay the paper on a flat surface. Remove the crust from a slice of white bread and knead the remaining into a soft wad. Gently rub this over the surface of the paper, rekneading as the "dough ball" becomes dirty.

Do Buy Old Frames That Nobody Else Wants

Sometimes you'll have the opportunity to buy empty frames by the handful. If they're in good shape you're likely to have to pay a premium for them, as people are always seeking nice frames. If they've deteriorated and look like a good prospect for kindling, however, you can usually snatch them up for next to nothing. I suggest you do that.

I especially urge you to buy composite or multiple-section frames — the ones that are commonly used for oil paintings and old photographic portraits. They're made up of two to four parts, all "nested" together to form the whole. In chapter 15, I'll show you how to resurrect almost any frame, sometimes in mere minutes.

Do Buy Beveled Mirrors That Are in Awful Condition

Are you beginning to see a pattern here? By now you should realize that much of what I'm telling you to buy is stuff that very few other dealers want. The fact is, if they knew some of the "tricks" that can transform these seemingly valueless objects into costly merchandise, if they knew how easy it can be, they would be competing with you. Fortunately for us, many people just won't take the time to learn these techniques or aren't willing to expend the minimal effort needed to get surprisingly good results. To put it bluntly, they're too lazy.

I veered off a bit with that explanation because I have to justify the fact that I'm now going to recommend that you buy something that comes very close to qualifying as junk.

When you look into a mirror and see nothing much more than spots and blotches and whatever's behind the mirror, you've located another possible addition to your growing inventory. If the silvering (the shiny stuff on the back that makes a mirror reflect) is falling off in huge patches, you're really in luck. In fact, the more that's gone, the better.

If you act on this seemingly weird advice, and the mirror you purchase is beveled, I promise to help you work some magic on it in chapter 15.

Do Buy Old Bottles

Buying and selling antique bottles won't pay your rent, but it might buy your lunch. *Smalls*, such as bottles, are important to have in your shop because you need a few interesting items that anyone can afford. They add variety at low cost without giving your shop that dreaded yard-sale look.

Bottles are a little like coins and stamps in that you've got to be an expert to recognize the ones that are truly valuable. Because of the huge quantities and nearly infinite variety of bottles that have been produced, you'd have to spend a lot of time to become an expert. But since the value of bottles is generally less than that of coins or stamps, you can afford to dabble in this collectible without becoming too well informed. You do need a little bit of knowledge, however. If "a little knowledge is a dangerous thing," then I'm going to make you really dangerous!

First, this is an item that you should only buy in bulk. When you can get a box full of dirty old bottles for a few dollars, pick it up. If an auctioneer or a flea-market dealer tries to sell you an individual bottle, it's highly unlikely that you'll be able to recover your cost.

Second, don't simply assume that a box lot of bottles has anything in it worth buying. If you haven't gotten your hands dirty and given the box at least a cursory examination, pass it up.

Dating Bottles

Although there are a lot of subtleties involved in dating bottles accurately, two items are useful indicators of age: (1) a *rough* pontil mark — this appears on bottles made until the middle-1800s; (2) a mold seam running from the base, up and through the lip — this indicates that the bottle was made after 1900; prior to that date, the lip was applied separately.

Which Bottles Sell Best?

As for desirability — that is, which bottles sell better than others — I've developed the following list of tips:

▸ Milk bottles are good only if they have the name and location of the dairy on them.
▸ Old bottles with their original paper labels are very collectible.

- Patent medicine containers that promise a cure for some ailment are eagerly sought.
- Bottles that are embossed (words pressed into the glass) are much better than those that are not.
- People tend to prefer unthreaded bottles unless the threads are on the inside, in which case the bottle was closed with a hard rubber stopper.
- Colors are better than clear glass.
- Clean bottles sell better than dirty bottles.

That last tip I sneaked in because I've got the neatest trick you've ever seen for scouring the interiors of filthy, old bottles: It's called *shotting*.

BOTTLES 101

Assuming you're not planning on opening Bottles-R-Us, all you really need is my crash course in bottle recognition and familiarity with the following terms:

a. **Base.** Bottom of the bottle

b. **Pontil mark.** An irregularity in the bottom of the bottle where the glassblower's rod, or pontil, was attached for handling during shaping

c. **Body.** The container part of the bottle

d. **Neck.** That long thing above the body

e. **Lip.** The opening at the top of the neck

f. **Mold seam.** The lines formed where the parts of the mold came together

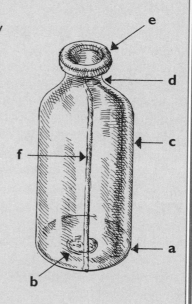

Shotting

A few years ago, while looking up a word in the dictionary, my eye happened to fall on the word *shotting*, used as a verb. Because the term sounded strange, I read the definition and stumbled on a really great cleaning trick. The definition read, "To clean a bottle by shaking with shot." I had struggled with bottle brushes, soaked bottles in bleach and detergent overnight, and tried running them through the dishwasher. None of these methods was very effective. When I used the shotting technique, I was amazed! Here's how:

1. Acquire a few ounces of steel shot, the smaller the better. These are the little pellets found inside a shotgun shell. Do *not* attempt to remove them from a live cartridge. Find a sporting goods store that sells reloading supplies or contact a gunsmith.
2. Pour the shot into the bottle with a little sudsy ammonia and water. A small funnel helps.
3. Shake the bottle vigorously while holding your finger over the top. The shot will scour the inside perfectly clean. Then pour the shot into the next bottle or pour it into a tea strainer to capture it for reuse.

Do Buy Handcrafted Furniture

Providing that they're well built and made from solid wood, handmade, one-of-a-kind pieces of furniture are safe buys. Much of this type of furniture was fashioned from "native" woods such as walnut, cherry, or pine, and often was made to fit a specific need or space. Because of this, you might have to be a little creative in coming up with suggestions for uses, but these custom pieces sell faster and for higher prices than their mass-produced counterparts.

The kinds of furniture I'm talking about here are *not* expensive, finely crafted pieces of furniture built by highly skilled artisans — such furniture is usually not within the price range of the average buyer. Rather, what we're looking for are items made by the slightly better-than-average carpenter or hobbyist of the late nineteenth or early twentieth century.

These creations might include toolboxes, magazine racks, medicine cabinets, blanket chests, or even "play" furniture for a child. Whatever their purpose, these unique items are imbued with a warmth and humanity that few can resist.

Do Buy Slip-Seat Chairs and Vanity Stools

Have you ever needed an occasional chair — just a simple, armless chair to use at a desk or a vanity, or for extra seating around the dinner table? Almost everyone does, occasionally. But finding a single, decent chair at a reasonable price is nearly impossible. For this reason, you should be the one who always has one in the shop.

What exactly is a "slip-seat" chair? It's one of those wooden chairs that has a single cushion attached by four screws, accessible from underneath. These little moneymakers can easily be reupholstered by a rank amateur in a matter of minutes. Usually you can simply stretch the new material over the old and staple or tack it in place.

Stop in at an upholsterer's shop and pick up a few scraps of nice material. They only need to be about eighteen inches square. Buy traditional patterns in neutral tones. Buy the good stuff. Most upholsterers are happy to get rid of these remnants at little expense to you.

By the same token, vanity stools with the same type of seat are constantly in demand. If I didn't consistently make 500 to 1,500 percent profit on these items, I wouldn't bother to tell you about them.

Do Buy Old Magazines and Illustrated Books in Poor Condition

Why buy magazines and books in poor condition? That's right. Let's all say it together: Because they're cheap! Because I love books, I can't in good conscience advocate destroying a good book just for profit. (There's a wealthy dealer in New York City who has been widely criticized for disassembling rare books in order to sell the individual prints contained in them. This is a case where the parts are worth a whole lot more than the whole.) On the other hand, old, not-so-rare publications in tatters are of little value intact. The illustrations and advertising "art" contained in them are worth salvaging, though. Usually, a periodical from the early 1900s will yield three or four prints that are suitable for framing. Most older books, which sometimes can be purchased by the box full, will contain at least one such picture.

Although this "found art" is an excellent way to use some of the frames that I advised you to buy, it's not always necessary even to go that far. If you don't happen to have the appropriate frame on hand, just back the prints with cardboard and cover them with plastic wrap for display in the shop.

DON'T OVERLOOK TEXTBOOKS

Old textbooks are often ignored by dealers, but they can provide artwork that appeals to people with special interests. Not long ago, I removed eight pages from a moldy old medical text and sold them as a set. Needless to say, the pictures, which probably hang in a doctor's office now, sold for many times what I paid for the entire box of books that this publication was in.

Do Buy Upholstered Furniture if the Fabric Is Shot

If the stuffing's hanging out, the covering is disgustingly dirty and stained, and the springs are sprung, you might want to consider this for your next purchase. As long as the frame is sturdy, the rest is of little consequence.

Most dealers won't touch this type of thing. Perhaps they have a misconception of what it costs to have a piece of furniture in such lowly condition refurbished. This is good news for you, since these candidates for the dump can usually be picked up for a few dollars.

Though having something reupholstered is by no means inexpensive, if it was originally a high-quality piece and the framework is sound, it's worth rescuing. But before you haul it off to the upholsterer's shop, save some money on the re-covering cost by doing a little of the unskilled labor yourself. (In chapter 16, you'll discover the secrets to getting the rock-bottom price on an upholstery job.)

When you buy an upholstered piece, do some of the dirty work yourself, and have a professional re-cover it, you can reasonably expect to double your investment. Normally, I like projects with a better return than that but, considering that we're talking several hundred dollars, I'll recommend it.

Do Buy Old, Tarnished Silver Plate

Here's another item that can be picked up for next to nothing. If the seller isn't practically giving the stuff away, don't bother.

I guess a lot of people are just too lazy to do the little work it takes to clean badly tarnished silver plate. You see it in shops all the time, dark and mottled. These dealers expect to make a profit for simply delivering these goods to their shops. Which would you rather buy if the price was the same — a dull, black teapot or the same item sparkling bright?

Frankly, I am one of the lazy! I'm too lazy to do all the laborious rubbing it would take to remove tarnish by the usual means. That's why I found a couple of nearly effortless methods to do it. (For specific details, see chapter 11.)

Since I'm going to tell you how to clean it, you should keep your eye out for it. Silver plate adds a touch of inexpensive elegance to your home or shop. Keep the following points in mind when buying tarnished silver plate:

- Check closely to see if the plating is intact. If it's been worn through to the metal underneath or is peeling off, no amount of polishing is going to save it.
- It's not a good idea to buy monogrammed or anniversary pieces. This severely limits the potential customers.
- Don't bother with forks and spoons but go for serving pieces, the more ornate the better. Teapots, creamers and sugars, pitchers, and trays are also quick sellers.

Do Buy Scrapbooks and Old Ledgers

There's an almost irresistible appeal to rummaging around in someone else's business. We may not like to admit it, but most of us are pretty nosy. Looking at what someone from the past felt was worth preserving gives us a chance to glimpse history on a personal level and to satisfy that streak of curiosity that's part of all of us.

Photo albums and albums filled with postcards are very desirable but usually aren't available at a reasonable price. Scrapbooks and ledgers normally fetch much lower prices but, in my opinion, reveal even more about every day life in the not-so-distant past. The trick to selling this type of material lies in how it's presented: Display it propped up and opened to an interesting page.

Do Buy Bridge Lamps

You've seen them in shops, at auctions, and in the background on television and in the movies. Everyone is familiar with them, but not everyone knows them by name. They're *bridge lamps*, and they have retained their popularity since they were first introduced sometime in the 1920s.

These lamps were manufactured in a variety of styles, from Victorian to art deco. All have a "head" that holds a single downward-pointing socket, and a heavy base. The column between the head and the base might be as simple as a painted steel pipe or as fancy as fluted brass with slag glass "breaks." More often than not, the whole lamp is of cast iron: head, base, and column (often just a twisted rod). Sometimes you'll see these lamps with wooden bases and columns, and a cast-iron or cast-brass head.

Originally, all of these lamps were fitted with paper or fabric shades that screwed onto the socket. The sockets were made with what is known as an *Uno* thread on the end, to accept those screw-on shades. Today, you'll see a lot of these lamps with glass shades attached. Since I believe in giving customers what they want, in chapter 14 I'll show you how to adapt a bridge lamp to receive a glass shade. I'll even show you how to convert a standard floor lamp to a bridge lamp and how to apply "believable" finishes. For now, don't worry about the terminology, rewiring, or refinishing. Just buy bridge lamps when they're cheap enough. The worse their condition, the cheaper they'll be, of course.

Do Buy Quality Lighting Fixtures and Table Lamps

Buying better-quality lighting fixtures and table lamps is good business. Really nice lighting is constantly sought by decorators and homeowners, and consistently sells well in any shop.

As a rule, higher-quality items consist of solid brass, while their cheaper counterparts are made of less costly materials, such as steel, and are then electroplated to look like the real stuff. While solid brass can be cleaned and burnished to a lovely, lustrous finish, attempting the same process on a plated object will usually remove the microscopically thin coating of brass and expose whatever is underneath. (In chapter 11, you'll learn the technique for cleaning and polishing brass, plus how to treat plated items.)

Is It Solid Brass or Plated?

A few years ago my wife and I decided to build a home that would incorporate some turn-of-the-century features known as "pan lights." These ceiling fixtures look sort of like two pie pans put together, with anywhere from two to five arms holding sockets and glass shades.

Our initial, very expensive purchase had been fully restored. That is, it had been rewired and the solid brass polished to a brilliant luster before being lacquered. The next light we found was "in the rough" and very inexpensive. We took it to a polishing shop (this was before I had learned to clean and polish brass myself) and had it redone.

Shortly after that we found another cheap one. This time, however, the proprietor of the polishing shop quickly informed us that it was not brass but simply brass-plated steel. How did he know?

From his shirt pocket he produced what resembled a ballpoint pen. Made something like a telescoping radio antenna with a powerful magnet on the end, it is a favorite of automobile mechanics, who use it to retrieve dropped nuts, bolts, and tools that fall into inaccessible engine recesses.

A telescoping, magnetic picker-upper clips neatly into your pocket.

Since brass is not magnetic and steel is, this instrument will help you to quickly distinguish the plated items from the solid brass ones. Of course some other metals such as "white metal" (an inexpensive alloy used in castings) are

> ## ANOTHER SIDELINE
>
> A lot of customers will pass up even good lamps if the lamps look like they need to be rewired. Because they're so much easier to sell when they're in safe, working condition, you should learn the simple procedure for rewiring that's explained in chapter 14.
>
> I started out rewiring the lamps that I sold. It was so easy, I started offering it as a service to other dealers and customers. I was surprised at the number of people who were afraid to tamper with anything electrical. Now I won't try to fix your TV, but anybody can repair a lamp. This little sideline might not buy new tires for your truck, but it's such easy money that I can't pass it up.

nonmagnetic also and will occasionally fool you. With a little practice you'll learn to recognize these impostors at least half the time.

Become Filthy Rich Without Lifting a Finger

Don't you wish? I have to tell you frankly folks, if you haven't already figured it out, that doing business my way means that much of your profit is earned through sweat equity. That means that you put in as little actual cash as possible and, through your own efforts (and ingenuity), increase the value.

The whole object of this book is to minimize those efforts and your cash outlay. It would be wonderful if I could predict exactly what will always sell for you, but I'm not clairvoyant. The thing is, if you find that some part of your inventory isn't moving as you think it should and you haven't sunk a lot of money into it, you're a lot less likely to become discouraged.

Although throughout this chapter I've encouraged you to buy things that need a little "help," don't take that to mean that's all you should buy. If you're out there looking, you will find bargains on the same items in good condition. Don't pass them up.

As you grow your business from the "backbone" inventory, you'll become more knowledgeable about what works best for you in your particular locale. Above all, though, remember this: If you're not having fun, you're not doing it right! Of course, it's a lot more fun when you can make some money at it.

▸5◂

getting good things for nothing

Use it up. Wear it out. Make it do or do without.

— Old New England maxim

Often the assumption is made that if something is free, it has no value. Generally speaking, that's a pretty safe assumption. But when it comes to the antiques trade, it's surprising how much salable merchandise and usable material you can obtain for little or no cost.

It's all a matter of knowing when and where to look, and more importantly, how to look. By "how," I mean the change in perspective that's developed by those who are successful in the antiques or, when you think about it, most any business that requires some degree of imagination and creativity.

You see, we all view the world differently. Looking at an old house, an architect notices the structure and design, an artist sees the colors, and a house painter might see only the peeling paint. An antiques dealer doesn't even see the house! Instead, the dealer imagines all the treasures that might be inside. What's in the cellar? What's in the attic? If you were the antiques dealer and you could see inside, would you recognize the potential value of objects?

In today's dangerous and distrustful world, you probably shouldn't go around knocking on doors, asking for a peek inside people's homes. But, undoubtedly, there *will* be situations where you'll get the opportunity to look at things that, without a good imagination, will seem of little value. If you begin now to make a conscious effort to look for the potential, rather than the immediately apparent worth, you'll have a tremendous advantage over most of your competitors.

Do You Want That?

In the first chapter, I talked about the boxes of miscellaneous items sold during most auctions and how these box lots often can yield good collectibles along with the junk. I also mentioned throwing or giving away most of the contents after extracting the few items worth keeping.

You simply can't keep all of this stuff, and ridding yourself of it at the sale is the best time to do it. If you take it home, you increase the probability of its taking up permanent residence in your storage space or "junking up" your shop. Sure it's painful. You hate to dispose of a usable spatula or a handful of pencils. But will you ever use them?

You'll find that many of the experienced buyers are practicing this box-lot shuffle during or after the sale. There's an opportunity here, because in the process, they make mistakes. I know this because I've made plenty. I realize it the moment I see the widening of the eyes and the uncontrollable grin appear when I answer, "No," to the casually asked question, "Do you want that?"

I guess you could always snatch it back quickly, but the honorable thing to do is let it go and try to learn something. Ask the person what it is that you've just given them. Most will be quite candid about it. It's hard not to gloat a bit when you just got lucky.

The good news is, you will recognize some things that others don't. Don't be shy. If you spot an item you want in a box that another buyer has just acquired, just ask the question, "Do you want that?" You might get growled at, but occasionally you'll be rewarded for your boldness.

More often than you might imagine, the box lot was purchased by someone who has no idea what's in the box, let alone the value of some of its contents. While you won't always be able to get the desired item for nothing, you might be able to buy it cheaply.

IF IN DOUBT, KEEP IT OUT

Once in a while in a box of odds and ends there will be an interesting item that you're just not sure of. It's all right to take this home if you promise yourself that you'll investigate it immediately. If you find yourself carrying "questionable" things home from auctions and allowing them to sit around for ages until you can get around to checking them out, you're going to find yourself buried in useless articles sooner than you think.

The Vultures Descend

The auction is over and the weary crowd is packing up and paying its bill. You're not finished yet, however. If you haven't walked away with some great buys, you've got one more chance for the ultimate bargain.

As I said, those who frequent these sales on a regular basis learn that they have to rid themselves of unwanted articles before they leave. The easiest way to do that is simply to leave it there. The typical scene at the end of the day will look like someone bombed a yard sale. There will be boxes, bags, and heaps of things that were jettisoned during or at the end of the auction.

This is one of the times my long-suffering wife likes to pretend she doesn't know me. You'll have to swallow a little pride to participate in the day's final activity, but there's way too much snobbery in this business anyway. Okay, there's no nice way to say this: You're going to pick through everyone else's discards.

You won't be alone, though. There are likely to be several resourceful individuals with the same idea. Most will be trying to retain some dignity by acting disdainful, idly poking at the "refuse" with the toes of their shoes. You might want to approach it that way, or you might go at it like I do: Jump in and get up to your elbows.

What to Salvage

I won't even attempt to list all the truly valuable goodies I've salvaged from the leftovers at auctions, but here's a little of what I want you to watch for:

- **Picture frames.** Some people discard them if the glass is broken or if they are a little damaged. In chapter 15, you'll see the wisdom of latching on to these.
- **Cracked or broken glass and mirrors.** If they're large enough to be cut down to fit smaller frames, you can use them.
- **Anything made of brass.** If you can't polish it and resell it, throw it in a box until you've collected enough to sell for scrap. Brass and copper are expensive!
- **Lamp parts.** This includes harps, bases, finials, sockets, nipples, threaded rods, and sockets. The lamp itself might be as ugly as sin, but most of its salvageable parts will be standard and reusable. In chapter 14, you'll learn to make use of them.

- **Old books and magazines.** In chapter 4, I recommended that you buy old books and magazines. After the sale many of them are discarded. The covers might be damaged, making them appear worthless. Are there any good ads, prints, or photographs in them, though? I made several hundred dollars framing and selling the lithographs from a book I once found in the middle of a parking lot. Several cars had already run over it when I rescued it.
- **Lampshades.** No one takes a torn, stained lampshade home, but the frames of some of them can be reused. Chapter 13 will instruct you in that simple procedure.
- **Old bottles.** Some collectible bottles are almost always left behind.
- **Anything that's broken that can be quickly and cheaply repaired.** Most people just don't want to bother.

PAY ATTENTION!

On my hall table I have a matching pair of handmade Weller vases that I bought at an estate auction. At that sale, one of the vases was on a table along with the china, crystal, silver, and the other more valuable smalls. The other was in a box of junk in the backyard.

I vied for the box with another buyer who was obviously very intent on acquiring its contents. I naturally assumed that she, too, was after the vase, since she topped my every bid without hesitation. I finally conceded defeat.

When the vase on the table eventually came up for bid, I was surprised that she was totally uninterested. Since she wasn't paying attention, she had missed seeing that I had to pay a lot for that vase. Well, I couldn't pass up this opportunity. I approached the lady, casually carrying my prize at my side.

"You've got a vase just like mine," I remarked. "It's a shame to break up a pair. Do you want to buy mine?" By now I was pretty sure that she couldn't care less about this ugly old vase. As I had hoped, she countered with an offer to sell hers to me. In the end, I acquired it at a tenth of what I had paid for its twin just fifteen minutes earlier.

I relate this story not to show you how clever I am but to show you how clever you must become. To get some of the best bargains, you've got to watch not only what's happening up front with the auctioneer but what's going on around you with the other bidders.

You've caught me at it again. I know I told you to dispose of all the junk that comes along with the things you intend to buy. And you're right, I'm now advising you to go picking through all the stuff that everyone else felt compelled to trash. The difference is that you're becoming more discriminating than the others. You're learning to recognize the potential.

House Haunting

You should get in the habit of haunting old houses: Keep your eye out for vintage houses and buildings that are being renovated or demolished. There's a pretty good market for architectural antiques and, surprisingly, many can be had for the asking. You'll need to get your hands dirty, but some of these artifacts can be removed easily with a few simple tools.

The first thing you need is, though, permission. Don't ever go into a house, even one that's being torn down, without permission from the owner. Aside from the fact that taking anything without permission is theft, the owner might fear liability if you get injured.

What's Worth Removing

If you can convince the owners that you absolve them of liability, and you are allowed to go in and salvage, there are a number of things you should look for:

▶ **Lighting fixtures.** Although a lot of older homes had their lighting updated at one time, many vintage fixtures remain in place. Chapter 14 gives you the information you'll need to restore them.
▶ **Fireplace mantels.** The majority of old mantels were simply nailed into place and can be pried away from the wall with little effort.
▶ **Claw-foot bathtubs and pedestal sinks.** Removing these could be too ambitious an undertaking for some, but they bring good prices in most areas. They're not that difficult to disconnect, but you'd better have a hand truck, a strong back, and a helper to tackle this project. You might want to see chapter 7 for a neat treatment for these tubs.
▶ **Ornate hardware.** By "hardware," I mean the fancy doorknobs, hinges, window latches, and switch plates commonly found in turn-of-the-century and earlier buildings.

Of course, if you have the storage space, a way to haul the stuff, the time and energy, and a little more ambition than I do, architectural elements like doors, shutters, and columns have a market also.

Watch for the "Sold" Sign

Moving is a traumatic experience. It's even worse when it's a do-it-yourself job. No matter how well they plan, people always seem to have more possessions than they have room for in the moving van. If they have the time or the inclination, they might have a yard sale prior to moving day. Naturally, you'll want to be first in line for that.

But it's the people who didn't have the moving sale that you need to approach. I don't like advocating taking advantage of people when they're vulnerable, but someone contemplating loading and unloading all of their possessions to and from a trunk might welcome an opportunity to leave some of them behind.

Some Approaches

When you see that someone's moving and you want to make them an offer on something, there are a number of approaches that work well:

1. **Tell them you're a dealer.** You're willing to buy, but you're sure not going to pay much. If they have ever considered selling that heirloom in the basement, now is the time they're most likely to do so.
2. **Just ask.** Do they have anything that they want to get rid of that they don't want to move? Certainly, they might see you as a freeloading bum, but take a chance. If their reaction is hostile, whip out a card and exclaim, "Oh! Did I forget to mention I'm a dealer? I mean, do you have anything you want to sell?"
3. **Offer to barter your labor.** This isn't for everyone, obviously. Packing and moving a household has to rank as one of the all-time least desirable jobs, but I have used this tactic in lieu of paying cash for something they've indicated they're willing to sell. I'll do almost anything to keep from dipping into the till.

TAKE A WALK

If you get the chance to salvage around an older home, remember to walk around outside while you're at it. Wonderful finds of considerable value could include wrought-iron gates and fencing; weathered birdbaths, feeders, and houses; and anything from the garden, such as flowerpots or cement urns.

I'll Trade Ya!

Since we're on the subject of bartering, we might as well take a close look at its applications in the antiques and collectibles trade. Personally, I think the trading of skills or labor between individuals should be practiced a lot more than it is.

If you're in the business, you'll find that most dealers pay to have at least some of their restoration work done by others. It might be furniture stripping or refinishing, lamp repair, pottery mending, frame repair, trunk restoration, reupholstery, or any number of other tasks that they can't or don't wish to do themselves.

Many of you possess one or more of these skills right now. If you don't already, with this book and a little practice, you will soon. I strongly recommend that you develop expertise in one or more of the many skills and crafts that dealers rely on. Not only will it come in handy in improving your own goods, but you'll be in a position to swap your work for merchandise or someone else's knowledge.

In chapter 4, I mentioned my sideline of lamp repair. Rarely does a week go by that I don't rewire a lamp for someone. In addition to that, if I chose to, I could spend most of my time restoring pottery and other ceramics for dealers. And although these dealers are quite willing to pay for these services, it can be advantageous to both parties if an exchange is made instead.

For instance, I can repair a lamp and charge ten dollars for my services or I can accept another defective lamp as payment. It's a good deal for both of us because the dealer paid very little for the second lamp. I'll fix it and sell it for several times what I would have originally been paid.

Not all of you will become adept at restoring ceramics, and very few of you are going to take courses in upholstering furniture (I did and found that it's one of those things I'll leave up to someone else), but *anyone* can rewire a lamp.

If that doesn't appeal to you, try seat weaving. Get some books or take an adult education class at a community college. Learn to cane chairs or do rush-and-splint replacement. That's a skill that's always in demand.

The point is, if you become expert in something that relates to the antiques business, your expertise and knowledge will be sought after. It's gratifying to be able to do something that others can't: It's useful for bartering, and it's a good hedge against the times when sales are slow.

Follow That Trash Truck!

A few years ago I visited a friend who is either smarter, more industrious, or a lot luckier than I am — he's considerably wealthier than I am, too. I deduce this from the fact that he resides in what we would consider as an affluent neighborhood.

I noted that day that on the curb, in front of several of the nice homes, were items that I could use. I recognized their potential value. Among them were a wing chair in need of re-covering, a small chest of drawers, and a number of floor and table lamps.

When I mentioned this to my acquaintance, he informed me that periodically the trash collection service in this community issues a notice that on a particular day large items can be placed at curbside for removal. So several times a year those rich folks drag their unwanted furniture and such to the sidewalk and wish it good riddance.

I hope this observation doesn't offend any readers, but the truth of it is, people who have a lot of money sometimes throw something away because they are just tired of looking at it. They could sell it, of course, but that's too gauche, too tacky. Besides, they simply don't need the money.

My buddy now lets me know when those collection dates are, and I make a point of being there the evening before or very early the morning of collection. By making a few phone calls I also got the schedules for several other communities and now make forays into these areas on occasion.

This won't become a primary source of merchandise, but it is one more opportunity to use your ingenuity to obtain something for nothing.

Visit Your Local Liquor Store

Sure, the antiques business can drive you to drink, but liquor stores can provide something you really need — the handiest containers you'll ever get your hands on: sturdy, partitioned boxes.

The compartments in these boxes vary in size to accommodate bottles of different diameters and heights. Pick up several to keep on hand. When you need to transport a number of fragile smalls, you'll find that most fit nicely into the divisions in the liquor boxes. The advantage to this system is that it eliminates the necessity of wrapping objects before you pack them. This will mean a lot if you've spent a long day at an antiques show or flea market and just want to pack up and go home.

The Cheap Seats

Where do you sit if you get tired at an on-premise estate sale? At many of them chairs aren't furnished, and seating on the furniture that's to be sold is limited. Aside from the fact that it's probably not going to be near where the glassware and other small items will be sold, it's going to be sold out from under you sooner or later.

You can carry a folding lawn chair with you but I've had them disappear on me when I've gotten up to look at something. Another option is a five-gallon plastic bucket. A bucket with a lid makes a comfortable seat. It's light and easy to carry around and serves several other functions.

When I'm going to an auction where I'm likely to encounter sparse seating, I tote my "auction bucket" along. In the bottom of the bucket, I place one of those ice substitutes that you freeze and reuse. On top of that, I might place our lunch and a couple of soft drinks. The rest of the bucket gets filled with paper or other packing materials. After I've consumed my snack, the glassware and other smalls I have bought are wrapped and placed in the bucket for easy transport home.

Five-gallon buckets are everywhere, so you shouldn't have any trouble acquiring one at no cost. Larger restaurants are a good source for these containers. A bucket you get from a restaurant will be fairly clean and won't contain any potentially harmful chemical residues, either.

See What the Boys in the Back Room Have

In chapter 4, I told you to buy chairs and stools with slip seats and advised you to go to upholsterers' shops in search of scraps and remnants. You also need to take a peek in the back rooms of a few other establishments.

Paint Stores

If you're going to do any of the faux finishing that you'll learn about in chapter 7, you'll need a variety of paints in various hues and colors. Those little bottles of acrylic craft paints are good for most jobs, but don't overlook the chance to get paint in larger quantities.

It might take you ten years to use a whole gallon, but if you can purchase the paint like this for less than what you would pay for a tiny bottle, why not buy it? The back room of a paint store is the source for this material.

Paint stores make mistakes, the most common being to incorrectly mix "custom" paint color. If it doesn't match what the customer ordered, it's practically worthless. Erroneously blended colors typically end up in some inconspicuous spot in the store like a stockroom; usually, you'll have to ask to see this selection.

And another thing: Don't hesitate to dicker on the price for this paint. They might have a reduced price on the can but that's just an attempt to recover their wholesale cost. Make them an offer. They've got to get rid of it, and since there's rarely enough of any one color to do an entire room, potential customers are few and far between.

The lighter colors are excellent for the base coats when marbleizing and sponge painting. The darker colors are useful for the intermediate steps. Naturally, they can all be tinted and intermixed to produce hues more suitable for the job at hand. In chapter 12, we'll explore more about mixing colors.

Wallpaper Shops

The next time you go by the wallpaper store, stop in and see what they have in discontinued patterns. If there are only a few rolls of a given design remaining, there's a good chance that you can pick them up at a drastically reduced price. Check out the borders, too. If you can find an inexpensive border that matches the wallpaper, you might be able to trim an edge off to use for restoring a trunk (see chapter 10).

Space, the Final Frontier

If you're now in the antiques business or have investigated the possibilities, you already know that next to the cost of your inventory, space in which to display and sell it is your biggest expense. If you're not quite ready to go into business on a big scale, there are some alternatives that can eliminate this expense altogether. I don't want to go into a lot of detail here because I'll cover this subject thoroughly in chapter 17. I will tell you, however, that there are two rent-free ways of presenting your merchandise to the public:

1. **Selling from consignment shops.** You just pay a percentage of the sale to the owner of the shop. This can be a big chunk of the money, however.
2. **Occupying display space in businesses where you'll pay no rent or commissions.** This one has you intrigued, doesn't it? Yes, there are businesses that will welcome your antiques and even sell them for you . . . for nothing (see chapter 17).

Take the Whole for the Parts

If I've accomplished anything in this chapter, hopefully I've opened your eyes to the possibilities of obtaining things that are of use and value to you but are most often overlooked by everyone else. If there's a trick to this, it may be in recognizing that even when you can't use the whole, you may be able to use the parts.

When you look at a lamp or a picture, you should see not the objects themselves but the finials and harps, the frames and glass. We dealers mentally dismantle, evaluate, and examine things we see. Once you begin viewing things from this perspective, it becomes an automatic response.

PART II

improving

If I were just starting in this business and I had purchased this book instead of written it, these next chapters are the ones I'd probably read first. This and the next part describe all those "tricks" that are used to improve and repair the antiques and collectibles that you buy.

Specifically, this section deals with improvements: cleaning, finishing, and enhancing the appearance of your antiques. I think you'll have fun with these chapters, and I know you'll discover some time-and-effort savers. For instance, you'll learn the formula for an old-fashioned, tried-and-true furniture cleaner as well as some unexpected newfangled ones. You'll see why people hate stripping furniture, but how you can make that job a lot easier. Marbleizing, sponge painting, and other faux finishing techniques are simplified for even the least artistic.

I'll guide you through the renovation of trunks, which are constantly in demand. Next, you'll find out that you don't have to work hard at cleaning brass, silver, or silver plate. Moreover, you'll find that many of the ingredients you'll need for cleaning are already in your pantry.

Let's roll up our sleeves.

▶6◀

cleaning wood furniture

At one time or another you've probably heard the physicians' code, "At least, do no harm." I think we antiques dealers should adopt this as our code and apply it to how we treat furniture when it comes into our shops. When I first started, the first thing I did when I brought a piece of furniture home was to drag it out back and slosh paint stripper all over it.

Later I realized that not only was it not necessary to refinish everything that came through the door, but that it wasn't even appropriate. A lot of that stuff was just plain dirty! Since then, I've taken a more conservative approach that saves me a lot of work and saves a lot of good finishes that are just hiding under layers of grime.

The Rules of Rejuvenation

If you apply these rules to each piece of furniture, you'll minimize your effort and everything in your shop will look great. Depending on the condition of the item in question, you should choose from four options:

1. **Do nothing.** That's the easiest one and the one a lot of dealers ignore. If the finish doesn't need any help, don't give it any! Just dust it and put it in the shop.
2. **Oil it or wax it.** If the finish is intact but just dull and "lifeless," a coat of wax is usually all that's needed. If the piece has a hard, high-gloss finish, I prefer an old-fashioned paste wax. On a low-luster piece, good old lemon oil works best.
3. **Clean it and then oil or wax it.** If the surface looks really bad, follow this procedure: If the finish looks "rough" and dull, it might still be salvageable. Don't resort to the stripper yet. Frequently,

what appears to be a "ruined" finish is simply years and years of accumulated dirt. One of the cleaners I suggest in this chapter might do the trick. At least try cleaning it first.

4. **Refinish it.** This really should be your last resort. If you've made a good attempt at cleaning it and find that there's just no restorable finish, then it's time to strip and refinish. Before you do that, however, read chapters 8 and 9.

Furniture Juice

Have you ever wondered what that aroma is in some antiques shops that sell a lot of wood furniture? It's pleasant but slightly pungent. The old oak in those shops seems to glow with inner warmth and feels silky to the touch. It hasn't been refinished; the patina is there, but it's so clean.

I remember to this day the very first antiques shop I went in, and the smells that greeted me and clung to my clothes for hours afterward. I've associated that odor with old wood and antiques ever since. But when I got into the business years later, I could never duplicate that smell.

A few years ago, I happened to be in a small shop somewhere in Indiana when that distinctive aroma wafted over me. I wandered to the back of the shop where the proprietor was busy scrubbing the daylights out of an oak sideboard. The smell was emanating from a Mason jar full of a milky liquid. Every so often, the owner picked it up, capped it, and shook it like a bottle of salad dressing. Then he would dip a piece of steel wool into the concoction and resume scrubbing.

This time I did what I should have done long before: I asked what he was using to clean his furniture. "Same old furniture juice everybody uses," he told me. "Just vinegar, linseed oil, and turpentine." He assumed that everyone knew about it.

To use furniture juice, just put the three ingredients into a jar with a tight lid and shake like crazy. Then use very fine (000 or 0000) steel wool to scrub the furniture. Don't be afraid to apply some pressure. You'll be pleased with how the years of grime melt away and how you're left with a smooth, clean surface.

Remember to shake the jar occasionally, as the ingredients tend to separate the longer they sit. Work on one area at a time. Don't apply it all over the piece and then rub, but rub as you apply it. When the surface is smooth, wipe it off with a soft rag. Ordinarily you won't need to use any wax or polish after this treatment.

Now don't go using this stuff on every item that you get — only those with badly soiled but salvageable finishes. I've tried a number of commercial wood cleaners, but I've never found one I like better.

THE FORMULA FOR FURNITURE JUICE

The formula for this wonderful wood cleaner and finish rejuvenator is simplicity itself:

- ▶ **⅓ white vinegar.** Apple cider vinegar might work but frankly I've never tried it, preferring to stick with what I know works well.

- ▶ **⅓ boiled linseed oil.** Don't use raw linseed oil. It won't dry but remains tacky when applied over another finish. You can get it at hardware and paint stores.

- ▶ **⅓ turpentine.** It used to be a popular paint thinner when everyone used oil-based paint. It's still available at paint and hardware stores.

Another Handy Cleaner

Every so often you'll get a piece that seems to have a pretty good finish, but when you try furniture polish on it, the surface seems sticky. This stickiness is usually caused by the environment the item has been in.

I once bought most of a houseful of furniture that must have spent fifty years closed up with a bachelor who smoked cigars, pipes, and cigarettes. I knew I had to clean it, and I figured the "juice" would work best. I decided to start on the smallest piece: a little mahogany magazine rack. As I was reaching for my jar of homemade cleaner, I knocked it over and spilled the little bit I had. Since I wanted to take the piece to the shop that day, I started looking around for a substitute cleaner.

On a whim I grabbed my can of hand cleaner (the type you use to remove paint and grease from your hands), dipped a pad of steel wool into it, and gently scrubbed the surface of the rack. To my delight the sticky tars that were coating the finish dissolved with my rubbing, and the piece wiped clean with a rag.

Since then, I've used this method for certain conditions, but I still prefer my "oil and vinegar" for most applications. Hand cleaners containing pumice work even better. As with anything else you put on a piece of wood, with hand cleaners you should exercise some caution. Hand cleaners contain solvents, and these can begin to dissolve some finishes. It's usually not a problem, but before applying it to a large area you should test it on that famous "inconspicuous place" that so many products talk about: It's better to be safe than sorry!

Oil Soap

Your furniture is dirty. So is mine. Like anything that sits in a house, dirt accumulates on it. What I like to do before I apply any kind of polish or wax is to wipe the piece with a cloth dampened with a solution of oil soap and water. Oil soap is commercially available and can be found on the shelf of your grocery store. If it weren't so cheap, I'd probably come up with a substitute for it.

My first "rule" notwithstanding, most furniture won't suffer from a going over with a little oil soap. It's formulated for wood surfaces, so it's not going to harm anything. This stuff makes things smell clean, too, so I always use some after I've done a piece with hand cleaner, which has an unappealing odor.

Sure, you are going to have some pieces that won't come clean. In those cases, chapters 8 and 9 will lead you through the messy world of refinishing.

marbleizing and other trick finishes

A few years ago I made a mistake that ended up being a good thing. Contrary to my own advice, I bought a dresser that had been painted. I stepped in the door at the auction, and couldn't resist: It was so cheap!

The second bit of common sense I ignored was not looking it over thoroughly before I bought it. Anyway, when I got it home I realized I was stuck. Not only did it have several layers of paint, but it was made of softwood and had loose joints, missing pulls, and, worst of all, deep gouges and holes in the top.

Any amount of paint can be removed, joints can be glued and clamped, and I can always find a set of drawer pulls in my box of miscellaneous hardware. Gouges and holes can be filled, too, but this particular piece just wasn't worth all that trouble. It appeared we would just have to take a loss on this one, and it wouldn't be the first piece I'd have to sell for half of what I paid for it.

Marbleizing and Sponge Painting

My wife, being the practical sort, suggested that we repaint the dresser and buy one of those marbleizing kits for the top. I had seen a few pieces done with one of those kits but wasn't terribly impressed. As well, the cost of the kit might end up being a case of throwing good money after bad if it didn't work.

Despite all this, I was intrigued by the faux marble finishing technique, so when I spotted an ad for a course offered at a local wallpaper store, I signed up. Basically this "course" consisted of paying fifty bucks to watch an expert produce realistic marble patterns on pieces of scrap wood. We students didn't get to do much marbleizing ourselves.

It looked simple enough, though, and later on, by following the basic principles and modifying some of the techniques, I found that I could produce a believable finish — a finish that fools the eye and covers a multitude of sins.

I know you're thinking that watching a process and reading about it are drastically different. Frankly I wasn't too sure I could describe this technique well enough for you to produce satisfactory results. So I experimented by providing a friend with the materials and a copy of my instructions. He was able to produce a reasonably good example on the first try. Since then, he's marbleized about half the objects in his house.

This proved to my satisfaction that any reasonably handy person can marbleize successfully. It will take a bit of practice. Don't expect the first piece to come out perfectly. The neat thing about marbleizing and its close relative, sponge painting, is that if you're not happy with the first try, you can paint over it and try again.

While the list of supplies may seem long, it's mostly things that you will be able to use on many other projects. I wouldn't have you buy a bunch of stuff for just *one* job, now would I?

Marbleizing Made Easy

Marbleizing is a wonderful way to "restore" furniture. Give it a try and see for yourself how easy it can be. These instructions may seem long and drawn-out at first glance. Keep in mind, though, that because these paints and finishes dry rapidly, you can easily complete a marbleizing project in a few hours.

MATERIALS & TOOLS

- Wood filler or epoxy putty (if needed)
- Fine-grit wet-and-dry, and medium-grit dry sandpaper
- Acrylic paint, white or off-white
- Acrylic paints, colors of your choice
- Foam paintbrush
- Empty coffee cans, a few
- Water

- Nubby cloth or natural sponge
- 2- or 3-inch synthetic bristle brush, cheap
- Feathers (chicken, duck, or bird), fairly stiff
- Rubbing alcohol (optional)
- Clear finish (water-based, acrylic "varnish")
- Fine steel wool
- Paste wax

---

1 Before you begin the actual marbleizing, you need to make sure the surface you want to finish is relatively smooth. Fill any deep scratches, holes, or gouges with a good wood filler or epoxy putty. (I like the putty because it dries fast, finishes like wood, and doesn't shrink.) The nice thing about marbleizing is that you don't have to remove whatever finish is on the piece in the first place. If there's missing veneer, or if there are cracks in the wood or other flaws, just fill them and sand the whole thing smooth with a medium-grit sandpaper. Then you're ready to begin.

2 Using your foam brush, apply a base coat of the desired color. This should be a very light color such as white, cream, or beige. You don't need complete coverage, just a fairly even coat. The first coat doesn't even have to be totally dry.

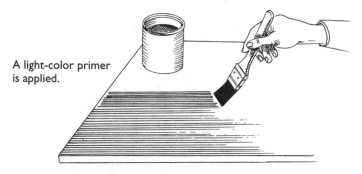

A light-color primer is applied.

3 Now you're ready to build up layers of color, beginning with a lighter hue and working up to a darker one (the darkest color will be the most prominent). In other words, if you want to duplicate a pink marble, begin with a pale pink and work up through successive shades, using at least three.

Put a little of the paint you're using into a container and add about twice as much water. You won't need much. About a tablespoon of paint will do a dresser top, for instance. Use a sponge or nubby material, such as a piece of knit sweater, cotton bathroom rug, or a section of a car-washing mitt cut to fit in the palm of your hand. Place this material in the paint to saturate it and then squeeze most of the paint out.

4 Dab the saturated cloth or sponge on the primed surface, attempting to keep an even pressure over the entire piece. Rewet the applicator as necessary and apply the paint as uniformly as you can. You don't have to be a fanatic about it. Irregularities will only add to the effect. You

Colors are sponged over the primed surface.

don't want to see rows of blotches, however, and be sure you don't cover the prime coat completely — you always want a little of this background to show through.

5 If, when you stand back and take a look, you see some areas that are a lot heavier than others, you can always lighten them by sponging a little of the diluted primer over them. None of this has to be perfect, remember. In natural marble, there are all sorts of variations. What you're striving for is the variation.

6 Repeat steps 3–5, using progressively darker shades, always leaving a little of the underlying colors visible. Each step will only take a few minutes, as the acrylics dry very quickly.

7 Now begins the detailing, the fun part where the surface suddenly "becomes" marble. Although you'll want to do a lot of the "veining" in white or cream, also add some really dark veins (see step 10). Go look at some real marble. Sometimes pink marble will have some brown streaks; a beige marble might have gray, green, or red striations.

Begin by selecting a fairly stiff feather. You can use artist's brushes instead of feathers, but brushes tend to make more regular lines, while a feather's stroke will be unpredictable and irregular, just the look you're trying to achieve. Dip the edge and tip of the feather into the slightly thinned paint and "draw" a few erratic lines completely across the surface, making them fairly thin but varying the width here and there. You can achieve a more realistic effect by pushing the feather at times. (The veins should be roughly parallel to each other but not parallel to any of the edges of the piece you're marbleizing.) Then, draw some very narrow lines branching off the main lines. They can be at any angle to the larger veins and can either intersect with other main veins or dead-end at any length. Remember, randomness is good.

Here again, you can't mess up too badly with this step. Just about any streak, smudge, or smear ends up adding to the overall effect, but restrain your artistic impulses and add only enough of these details to achieve a marblelike appearance. More is not necessarily better.

Details like veins are added with the tip of a feather.

8 Once in a while, dip the tip of the feather into a half-and-half mixture of rubbing alcohol and water, and run it along a portion of a line while the paint is still wet. This will cause the paint to blur and spread a bit, and will mottle the color somewhat. Add a tiny touch of contrasting color while doing this, so it can "bleed" into the other paints.

9 Thin the paint a little more and, using the flat surface at the tip of the feather, make a few "smears" that are only about two inches long and half as wide. The paint should be thin enough to allow the underlying surface to show through. These smudges can be placed anywhere on the piece but are particularly effective located at an edge.

10 For the final touch, add "flaws" that mimic what you commonly see in real marble. For this step, select a darker contrasting color and make some short squiggly lines that run at angles totally different from the general direction the main veins are running in. These "flaws" can cross any of the lines you've drawn, but they should be placed completely at random. Be careful not to place them in any sort of pattern.

Make one line at a time, and use the alcohol-and-water mixture to blur some of the edges. Make as many or as few as you like, but moderation in adding these details will result in a more realistic appearance.

11 When your piece is totally dry, brush on a coat of a clear finish with your foam brush. For best results, use nothing other than a quick-drying vinyl or acrylic varnish. The advantage to these products is that they can be wet sanded in about a half hour. (I don't like to tout too many brand names, but in the back of the book I'll let you in on my favorite finishes as well as a few other useful products.)

12 Using a wet-and-dry paper of about 400 grit, sand the surface in a circular motion. Apply quite a bit of pressure, rewetting the paper often. Next, wipe the surface with a damp cloth and then a dry one to remove the sanding residue.

13 Repeat steps 11–12 at least three times, until you have a perfectly smooth-to-the-touch finish.

14 Finally, rub the whole thing down with very fine steel wool and paste wax. Buff the surface afterward, and you'll swear you're looking at and touching a slab of marble.

ITEMS YOU CAN MARBLEIZE

Once you get the hang of it, you'll want to practice this craft often. Don't stop with furniture tops, though. Here are a few suggestions for other items that look good with this treatment: claw-foot bathtubs, windowsills and doorsills and baseboards, lamp bases and columns, bathroom and powder room walls, picture and mirror frames, fireplace mantels, flowerpots, and entire floors.

Sponge Painting

Congratulations! You already know how to sponge paint, if you've tried the marbleizing. Think of sponge painting as marbleizing minus a couple of colors and all of the detailing. I often combine this process with marbleizing on the same piece of furniture, since it works especially well on the legs of tables and stands.

One nice thing about sponge painting is that you don't have to prepare the surface much before you paint it. The irregularity of the splotches made by this method works like camouflage. By breaking up the visible outlines of flaws, such as dents and scratches, they are somewhat concealed and so disappear from view. Of course, really deep inperfections should be filled and sanded before painting. Unsalvageable items *can* be salvaged!

First you have to decide on the color combination. Ninety-nine percent of the sponging I do on furniture is in black and various shades of brown. The shade of brown you pick can range from one that's nearly as dark as the black to one that approaches orange. By varying the color, you can simulate anything from walnut to mahogany to tortoiseshell. By changing the background color from black to something like tan, and substituting black or very dark brown for the sponging color, you can approach a finish that resembles bird's-eye maple. Let your imagination — and what you see around you in natural woods — be your guide.

OIL AND WATER

Oil and water don't mix, right? Well, stick with me folks, and we'll defy the laws of chemistry! It's perfectly all right to apply the base coat with oil-based paint and to sponge on the other color with an acrylic water-based paint, preferably while the oil paint is still wet. You can even reverse the order of oil- and water-based paints in your application. What? You think this combination isn't going to dry? Of course it will — it just takes a little longer. Relax. Go have a cup of coffee. Come back and look at it tomorrow.

- Paint, two colors, or two shades of the same color
- A paintbrush for the base coat and the finish coat (if needed)
- A natural sponge or nubby cloth
- A clear acrylic or vinyl varnish (if needed)
- Foam paintbrush
- Sandpaper, 400-grit wet-and-dry

1 Brush on your first coat, the background color. You want pretty good coverage, but it doesn't have to be a super paint job. Don't be overly concerned with visible brush strokes. Just give it a quick going over, but watch for runs and drips. Better too little paint than too much.

2 Dip a piece of nubby material or a natural sponge lightly into your chosen color of unthinned paint. Don't saturate it; you just want a little bit of paint on the surface of the sponge.

3 Gently pat the surface with the sponge, transferring just the amount of paint needed to achieve the effect you're seeking. You can cover as little or as much of the background as you like. It's better to go a little easy on it at first and then, if you think it needs more coverage, go back over it and add more.

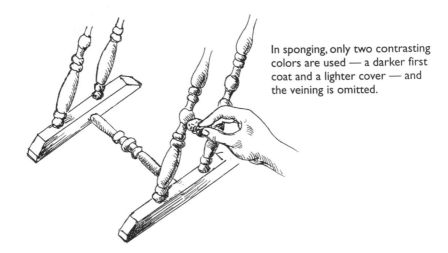

In sponging, only two contrasting colors are used — a darker first coat and a lighter cover — and the veining is omitted.

4 Steps 1–3 take all of ten minutes, so you're practically finished. If you used flat paint, you'll have to go over it with one or two coats of the clear finish. Use a quick-drying acrylic or vinyl varnish applied with a foam brush.

5 Sand the surface with a 400-grit wet-and-dry sandpaper, rewetting the surface often. Wipe with a damp cloth and then a dry cloth.

6 Repeat steps 4–5.

This technique is pretty quick, but for even faster sponging here's a little hint: If you use a low-gloss (not flat) acrylic enamel, you might get by without having to put a clear finish coat over the sponging. I don't recommend this for large, flat surfaces, but it works fine on legs, spindles, and such.

SUITABLE SUBJECTS FOR SPONGE PAINTING

This technique is so quick and easy, you'll find yourself using it on more things than you can imagine. Here are few ideas to get you started: picture and mirror frames, entire chairs (gives a cheap, yard-sale find a formal, classy look), whole rooms, table legs, lampshades, wastebaskets, and wooden boxes (transforms an inexpensive little box into one that resembles an early-nineteenth-century "deed" or document box).

Grain Painting

Graining, or grain painting, has been around for ages. Traditionally, it has been used to disguise low-cost materials by making them resemble better-quality wood. Done by a professional, that type of graining is hard to detect. If you ever get a chance, look at the doors in Thomas Jefferson's home, Monticello, for some wonderful examples.

Other types of graining became expressive, with no attempt to exactly reproduce the patterns seen in a real wood surface. This type of decoration was more in line with what the average person could accomplish, and was widely practiced by eighteenth- and nineteenth-century craftsmen to embellish their homes and furnishings. Today, good examples of this work are prized more highly than those that received the traditional, trompe l'oeil ("fool the eye") graining.

What I'm going to show you is the more decorative form of the craft — not because it's more attractive (although it is), but because it's downright easy! We'll look at two simple techniques: feather painting and modeling-clay graining.

Feather Painting

For this method, you're probably going to need a couple of feathers, bcause you should change to a fresh one when the first gets saturated with paint. Feathers are everywhere: friends bring me feathers, I pick them up around my bird feeders, and a couple times a year I make a trip to a nearby city park that has lots of ducks.

In grain painting, you'll reverse the order of colors that you use in sponging. For example, if you were to apply a black base coat on the legs of a table and then sponge on brown, the opposite would be true when graining.

MATERIALS & TOOLS

- Foam paintbrush
- Paint, two colors (one is usually black), oil or water based
- Left wingtip feathers of a northbound Canada goose (actually, any fairly stiff feathers)

- A clear acrylic or vinyl varnish
- Sandpaper, wet-and-dry
- Steel wool
- Paste wax

---

1 Brush on a coat of the lighter color paint (a foam brush is ideal), covering well. Allow that coat to dry. It's best if this base coat is a flat paint.

2 For the actual grain pattern, the trick to an attractive design is uniformity. Dip the feather's tip and edge into the paint and make a row of sweeping arcs, one below the other, across the surface you're graining. It works best if you start from the inside of the arc and make a sweeping motion to the outside. Leave a narrow space and then paint another row alongside the first, again starting from the inside and sweeping outward.

3 Repeat this process over the entire surface of the object that you're painting. It's important that you try to keep the design fairly uniform and your rows approximately parallel to the edges of the object being grained. If you'd like, you can reverse the direction of every other row of arcs. This is advisable on larger surfaces but isn't appropriate on narrow items, such as picture frames.

A series of arches is drawn with the top of a feather. The next row of arches can be upside down.

4 After completing your pattern and letting it dry, coat the surface with a clear acrylic finish.

5 Wet-sand the surface and rub it down with fine steel wool and paste wax. You can omit the sanding and rubbing if the surface isn't going to get much touching, but otherwise the feel of the finish is important.

Modeling-Clay Graining

This is, by far, the simplest and fastest method of graining you'll find. It's a little messy, and the materials are a bit bizarre, but as with the other faux finishing techniques, practice is all you need.

MATERIALS & TOOLS

- Background paint (a light color such as beige), oil or water based
- White vinegar
- Sugar
- Plain old children's modeling clay

- Rubber gloves
- Powdered, water-soluble aniline stain.*
- A clear acrylic or vinyl varnish
- Sandpaper, wet-and-dry
- Steel wool
- Paste wax (if needed)

*Furniture "powders" — finely ground pigments used for making stains — can be substituted. (If you can't find these products locally, see the sources list.)

---

1 Coat the surface with a flat, neutral-color background paint. (You don't have to use a lighter, neutral base coat if you don't want to. For your first try, though, it's a good idea because with a neutral base it's easier to see the effect you're getting.) Allow this coat to dry.

2 Warm about a cup of the vinegar and dissolve sugar in it until you get a thin syrup. (Don't boil it — you're not making candy.) It might take as much as half a cup of sugar, more or less. Pour this into another container and add a little of the powdered stain, probably less than a teaspoon, until you get a deep, rich color.

AN ALTERNATIVE TO VINEGAR AND SUGAR

Although the vinegar and sugar is an old, traditional formula, the powders can also be dissolved in acrylic varnish. It tends to dry fast, so you can't fool around once you start.

---

3 Take a hunk of the modeling clay and twist it into a rope that's as long as the width of your hand and as big around as, say, a carrot. You want it lumpy and irregular in shape, not smooth.

4 Pour some of the "syrup" into a shallow dish (I like to use paper plates because they're disposable), and roll the clay, as you would a paint roller, through the mixture. (Wear rubber gloves because you'll never get this stuff off your hands.) Then, simply roll the clay across the primed surface that you're decorating. Repeat the process until the surface is covered. After each pass, you may want to wipe the clay off a little. You can also retwist it occasionally to vary the pattern that it's laying down.

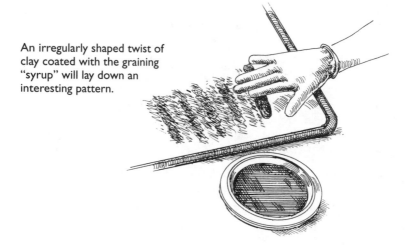

An irregularly shaped twist of clay coated with the graining "syrup" will lay down an interesting pattern.

5 After you've allowed the graining to dry thoroughly — this can take quite a while — coat it with a clear varnish.

6 Wet-sand it and rub it down with fine steel wool, and paste wax.

THINGS TO GRAIN PAINT

The list is practically endless, but a few of my favorites are: tin trunks, almost any piece of furniture, picture and mirror frames, boxes, and fireplace mantels.

▸8◂

if you absolutely must strip

Most books I've read on furniture finishing tend to breeze through any discussion of *stripping*, or finish removal. Maybe it's because the subject's so boring. You already know that I'm not a fan of stripping, that I consider it a last resort. But since I'm cheap, there are times when cleaning just won't do the trick, and something really nice can be had reasonably, precisely because it needs to be refinished.

With all this in mind, you should know something about strippers, how to use them, and their pros and cons. I classify the basic types as wash-off, scrape-off, slow-acting "safe" strippers, and re-amalgamators.

Liquid vs. Paste Removers

Within the categories of wash-off and scrape-off strippers, you have a choice of liquid or paste varieties. One isn't better than the other, but they do have slightly different uses.

Liquid stripper has the advantage of allowing you to continually "flood" the surface and to collect and reuse the stripper that runs off. Commercial stripping operations use this type. I like liquid stripper for varnished and lacquered pieces because the finish is dissolved, liquefied, and flushed off the surface. Its disadvantage is the same as its advantage: Specifically, it runs off. Liquid stripper won't stay put on a vertical surface, so you'll need to apply and reapply.

Paste or semi-paste removers stick to whatever surface they're applied to. This gives them the advantage of sitting there and working while you go off to read other sections of this book. The disadvantage of paste or semi-paste removers is that whatever you put them on has to be scraped off. Also, you cannot collect and reuse what is scraped off.

Be Cautious

We might as well get the cautions out of the way early on. I know this information is on the label of the stripping products, but who reads all that fine print?

1. **Don't do this job indoors!** I save all my stripping jobs until the weather allows me to work outside. Except for the "safe" strippers on the market (which we'll discuss later), assume that all strippers are flammable and explosive, and that the fumes are hazardous to your health. Regular face masks (or respirators) won't protect you from toxic fumes. In fact, they can trap fumes and be more dangerous. Good ventilation is an absolute *must.*

2. **Wear protective gear!** Most of these products would just as soon take a layer off your skin, as a layer of paint. If it's not strong enough to burn you, it's not strong enough to work effectively as a stripper. Be sure to wear a long-sleeve shirt or arm protectors and rubber gloves.

3. **Don't burn down your house!** The rags that you use will contain residue of the finishes as well as the stripper. They have been known to ignite spontaneously. Don't dispose of the rags in a container in the house or even near the house. In fact, it's best to put the used rags in a container that contains water. There are so many federal and local laws governing the disposal of potentially toxic waste and they change so often, you should contact your local waste collector for approved disposal procedures in your area.

Wash-Off and Scrape-Off Strippers

When you see a remover described as "wash-off," it doesn't mean that you can put the stripper on and then stand back and spray both it and the old finish off with a blast from a water hose. I wish it were that easy! Some people avoid using scrape-off removers because they sound like they're going to involve more work than wash-off varieties. In fact, because there's generally more work involved preparing, staining, filling, and finishing a piece that's been stripped with the wash-off method, the overall effort and time required is probably less with the scrape-off formula.

The wash-off method can be quicker, though, notably when used on pieces that you're not too particular about, and especially if you're not planning to put a super finish on it, and the piece isn't worth putting a lot of effort into. Sure, you should knock the "whiskers" raised by the water off the surface with fine sandpaper, and you might give it a coat of stain if it's needed, but don't fill the grain or worry yourself to death about getting a perfect finish on these pieces.

On the other hand, if the quality of the piece justifies an excellent finish, I always recommend the scrape-off remover. It does less damage to the piece, so there is less for you to take care of in the finishing stage.

MATERIALS & TOOLS

- Long-sleeve shirt or arm protectors
- Chemical-resistant gloves (PVC-coated is best)
- Large pan or tray (optional)
- Stripper
- Container to put stripper into
- Cheap "real" bristle brush (some synthetic bristles dissolve)

- Scraper
- "Stripping" brush for scrubbing
- Coarse, medium, and fine steel wool or stripping pads
- Water (addition of a little laundry detergent is optional)
- Rags
- Denatured alcohol, lacquer thinner, or paint thinner

1 Put on a long-sleeve shirt or arm protectors, and wear protective gloves.

2 Place the piece to be stripped on a large pan or tray (if available), and pour the stripper into a container like a large coffee can.

3 Apply the stripper liberally with a bristle brush. The biggest mistake people make is not using enough stripper. It might seem wasteful, but by not skimping on the product, you'll more than make up for its cost in time and effort saved. Working from the container and the run-off that collects in the tray, keep the surface wet. Continue putting the stripper on until the finish begins to wrinkle (if it's paint) or dissolve (if it's a varnish or lacquer).

4 Scrape off as much of the mess as you can. Use a plastic drywall "joint" knife for flat surfaces, and your stripping brush, which has soft plastic and copper bristles, for the nooks and crannies. (If you're using wash-off stripper, you're not ready to wash it off yet.)

5 Apply more stripper with the bristle brush. Sorry, but one application of remover rarely does the whole job. With this coat, you'll need to work it in and scrub the surface with steel wool or a stripping pad saturated with the stripper. Use the stiff-bristle brush for those crevices. Don't rub too hard or you'll damage the surface.

Plenty of stripper is applied, keeping the surface wet until the paint begins to wrinkle or the varnish starts to dissolve. Most of the old finish is removed with a plastic scraper.

SAVING THE STRIPPER

I like to get as much use out of a purchase as I can. Because any liquid stripper that runs off is still pretty potent, capturing at least some of it and reusing it only makes sense.

A few years ago I bought some big pans and trays at a restaurant auction. Most furniture won't fit in these trays of course, but I can usually arrange a few to catch a portion of the stripper that might otherwise be lost. A restaurant supplier might sell you a couple of trays at wholesale.

6 If you're using wash-off stripping, now you're ready to wash everything off. I prefer to use a bucket of soapy water and coarse steel wool for this task. Scrub the piece down, rinsing your steel wool in the bucket occasionally. Spray the piece with a water hose and scrub with clean, medium steel wool or a stripping pad. Wipe it down with dry rags and allow it to dry.

Remaining stripper and finish are scrubbed off with soapy water and steel wool.

If you're using scrape-off stripper, keep repeating step 5, wiping the piece off between coats with clean rags, until the old finish is gone but the underlying stain and filler are still intact.

7 When the piece is dry, use some lacquer thinner, denatured alcohol, or paint thinner, and fine steel wool or a rag to remove the final traces of finish.

PROS & CONS

WASH-OFF STRIPPERS

+ Remove finish thoroughly, including most of the underlying stain
+ Strippers do most of the work
− Wood and water can mean trouble; water raises the grain and can loosen veneer and glue joints
− Can remove much of the grain "filler" that gave a porous wood its smooth finish
− Restaining may be necessary
− Long drying time (as much as 8 hours) before finish can be applied; drying time can vary, depending on type of wood, individual piece, and humidity.

SCRAPE-OFF STRIPPERS

+ Remove the old finish, but allow more control: retains stain and grain filler
+ Don't raise grain
+ Usually won't loosen glue joints or veneer
− Takes a bit longer to remove old finish
− Require several applications and more stripper

Safe Strippers

I was hesitant to talk about this slow-acting product because, as you know, I want to get the job done quickly. I got thinking about it, though, and realized that my main objection isn't really valid. The stripper itself takes a long time to work, but you don't put in any more time than you would with any other remover.

MATERIALS & TOOLS

- Newspaper or something to catch residue
- Stripper
- Container to hold stripper
- Brush for application
- Plastic wrap
- Scraper

- Coarse and medium steel wool
- Coarse stripping brush
- Rags
- Soapy water
- Denatured alcohol, lacquer thinner, or paint thinner

---

1 Place the piece on newspaper to catch stripper residue, and pour some stripper into a large can or other container.

2 Apply the stripper liberally, brushing on a thick coat. (With this product, you don't want to work a small section at a time.) Now go fishing or something. If you're removing a clear finish such as varnish, it's going to take at least an hour to work. If it's paint, you should cover the surface with a "skin" of plastic wrap, if possible, and go fishing somewhere far away, because 12 hours is about average for this job.

3 After the stripper has had time to do its job, scrape the loosened finish off. Use coarse steel wool or a stripping pad and the stiff-bristle stripping brush to remove the residue from the nooks. Repeat this process if there's more finish to remove.

4 Scrub the piece down with rags soaked in soapy water. Read the manufacturer's directions before you do this. As of this writing, the only "safe" strippers on the market are wash-off.

5 Do one final cleanup with medium steel wool and solvent (the alcohol or thinner).

6 Let the piece dry thoroughly.

SAFE STRIPPERS

+ Considered "safe" because they don't irritate your skin (so you don't need to wear protective gear), fumes aren't damaging to your health, and it isn't flammable or explosive; rags and residue must be disposed of safely, though
+ Can be used indoors; ideal for apartment dwellers or when weather doesn't permit use of other types of strippers outside
− Takes a long time
− Rather expensive when compared to other varieties

Re-amalgamators

That sounds more like a name for a group of superheroes on a Saturday morning cartoon show than a descriptive term for finish removers, doesn't it? In fact, if you go into a hardware store and ask for it by that name, they probably won't know what you're talking about.

Often you'll see this product packaged as an expensive kit or referred to as a "refinishing liquid" rather than a finish remover, the idea being that you can strip a piece of furniture without *really* stripping it. That is, if the original finish is intact but in poor condition, you can dissolve and re-amalgamate (or remix) it.

I'm not going into any detail about this product because I don't think it fits into my overall concept of doing the job in the fastest and least expensive manner. Re-amalgamating "refinishers" have their place among do-it-yourselfers who do an occasional piece but not, in my opinion, in the shop of a dealer who's doing "production" work. If the finish on a piece is not bad enough to justify removing it completely, you should just clean the piece up and sell it!

Some General Advice to Save You Money

As always I don't want you to spend any more money than you have to, so here are a few hints about finish removers in general:

- **Buy the store brand.** Read the labels. The effective strippers (other than "safe" types) are all made of the same ingredients: Methylene chloride and methanol do the work, and things like toluol and acetone affect their penetration, drying, and neutralization properties. So the store brands will usually be as good as the more expensive brands.

- **Buy in bulk.** If you're going to do a fair amount of stripping, you'll be a lot better off buying in bulk from a supplier. I even buy it in quantities large enough to sell a few 5-gallon containers to other dealers (another little sideline). See the Sources at the back of the book for suggestions.

- **You can never have too many rags.** Since you need lots of rags, don't pass up those cheap linens that no one else wants at auctions. Also, if you live near a clothing manufacturer, you can get rags inexpensively. Ask your friends to save their old clothing for you instead of throwing it away.

- **Use stripping pads.** These pads are made of a synthetic material and, unlike steel wool, can be used over and over.

- **Don't buy special stripping gloves.** PVC-coated gloves found in grocery, hardware, and auto supply stores are cheaper and just as good.

- **Use lots of stripper.** No, I'm not a stockholder in any of the companies that make it, but I've found that my time is usually worth more than the products I use, and skimping on finish removers will only cost you time.

▶9◀

refinishing

The *American Heritage Dictionary* defines the word *finished* as "smooth and polished, as wood." It's also defined as "undone; destroyed; ruined." Believe me, I've seen more of the latter than the former.

In the introduction to this book I told you that this wouldn't be another furniture-refinishing manual, and it certainly isn't. There are any number of good books in print that delve deeply into the "art" of the perfect finish. If refinishing is going to be your "bread and butter" in the antiques trade, you'll need to study some of them. For the rest of you who are interested in obtaining a "nice" finish that you'll be proud of but don't want to make refinishing a career, stick with me. I'll get you through it without spending a heap of money on equipment or materials.

Even if you never intend to refinish a piece of furniture, there's information in this chapter that you need. You'll learn about finishes and finishing techniques that you'll use on things other than furniture.

FIRST ADVICE

▸ **Use proper precautions when applying any kind of finish.** Read the label. If it says to allow for plenty of ventilation, do it. When you're spray painting you need ventilation, but you should also wear a respirator. As with stripping, I try to do a lot of this outdoors.

▸ **Start small.** Begin with a fern stand instead of a dining room suite.

▸ **Don't be afraid to experiment.** Anything you do wrong is correctable. You don't need talent, only practice.

There's probably no other subject in this business that elicits more "expert" advice than refinishing. Almost everyone will recommend a specific product or technique. I've got my preferences, and some of you purists out there won't agree with all of my suggestions. The one thing even the pickiest refinisher will agree with me on, however, is this: Preparation of the surface prior to application of the finish is one of the most important steps, so let's start there.

Should You Sand?

You may have noticed that there was very little said about sanding in the previous chapter on stripping. You might, then, expect me to discuss this subject at some length here. I do have some advice on the subject, but it mostly boils down to don't! Or, at least, don't do much.

Few occasions in refinishing antiques require the use of sandpaper. If you've stripped the furniture properly, only light sanding is needed after using wash-off strippers and between coats of finish. I'm constantly dismayed by the unconscionable use of sandpaper and electric sanders on what otherwise would be good, salable furniture. I've seen veneer sanded through, and waves, gouges, and other damage inflicted by well-meaning but misguided refinishers. Some refinishers seem to think they must remove all traces of previous use: This might be true if you're repainting an automobile, but it doesn't apply to antiques. In fact, signs of wear often add to the appeal of some antiques.

SAVE ON SANDPAPER!

▸ When you purchase a sander, make sure it uses a fourth of a sheet of sandpaper, so you can buy whole sheets and cut them to fit. Otherwise, you'll spend more to purchase odd-shaped, precut sheets.

▸ Don't buy a sander that uses adhesive-backed paper. That stuff's really expensive. If you do end up with one of those, make your own sheets by coating the back of regular paper with spray adhesive.

Electric Sanders

The fact that power sanders aren't necessary to refinish furniture should be good news. But if you absolutely must own an electric sander to feel that your life is complete, make it a "finishing" or oscillating type, not an orbital sander. The two sanders look the same, so you've got to read the description of their "action."

Oscillating vs. Orbital Sanders

The working surface of an oscillating sander moves in a straight, back-and-forth motion — the proper motion for sanding with, or in the direction of, the grain. The action of an orbital sander, on the other hand, leaves little circles in the sanded surface, partly because its motion causes it to be sanding against the grain for a portion of each of its tiny "orbits."

Detail Sanders

If you insist on using power sanders, you might as well buy a *detail* sander while you're at it. This tool has a small, triangular head that can get into hard-to-reach places (like between the spindles on a chair back) that other sanders can't. I wouldn't even recommend this machine if it didn't have another useful function: The sanding head can be removed and replaced with a scraper head. Although you won't use this feature often, there will be times when you'll find an electric paint scraper useful.

An oscillating sander *(left)* sands with the grain. A detail sander *(right)* will get into difficult spots and doubles as a power scraper.

Hand Sanding

I contend that hand sanding should be adequate for 99 percent of the refinishing work that antiques dealers do. If it's not, then you're probably buying the wrong furniture. Even when sanding by hand, there are decisions to be made.

Sanding Blocks

To sand flat surfaces, you need a sanding block. To make a sanding block, you'll need a block of wood that's 3 inches by 5 inches, and about 1 to 1½ inches thick. Glue a piece of felt (available in craft stores) to the bottom of the block to act as a cushion. Cut a standard 9- × 11-inch sheet of sandpaper into quarters, then simply fold the sandpaper around the block and hold it in place. There's no need to fasten the sandpaper to the block.

Sanding Sponges

I love these things. If you're not familiar with them, they're made from a dense foam material and have abrasive on all four sides — usually a medium grit on one side and edge, and fine on the other. They're firm enough to act as a sanding block but flexible enough to get into contours.

Sanding sponges are nearly indestructible. I generally get a year's use out of one. They're also washable, so when they become clogged with wood dust, simply rinse them out.

Kinds of Sandpaper

Sandpaper can be confusing: flint, aluminum oxide, silicon carbide, 150 grit, 220, 400. Do you need some of each? Let's keep it simple. Make or buy a sanding block for most work, and get some 220 and 400 wet-or-dry paper. That's it! If you can't remember that, then just remember "fine" and "very fine."

Either by hand or with an oscillating sander, sand bare wood with fine paper (using it dry) before applying finish. After that, between coats, use very fine (or fine again if there are noticeable brush marks) wet.

Between coats, don't use a power sander, and don't apply much pressure. Both create friction and heat, which can soften the finish.

Staining

Almost anything you've stripped is going to need some staining. Oil-based, wax-based, and water- or alcohol-based aniline stains can do the job. You should eliminate the aniline stains from your list of possibilities right away, since they're only useful when the wood has no remnants of the old finish; their application can be a little tricky for the novice, too.

That leaves oil- and wax-based stains. Generally speaking, you probably shouldn't use oil stains much, either: They dry slowly and can be difficult to work with.

Wax stains are your best bet. They penetrate well and are easy to apply. Sometimes you can even get by without applying a finish coat over them. Wax stains are ideal for beginners and for people like me who don't like to do unnecessary work.

Applying Stain

Applying stain is easy: Just dip a disposable foam brush or a rag in the stain and apply it over all the surface. As you work, go back and wipe off any excess before it begins to dry. You can apply additional coats if you want a darker finish. After that, you're ready to topcoat with varnish or simply buff up the surface with a soft rag. In many cases, especially with oak, that's the entire process. No finish coat is needed, and you're left with a nice hand-rubbed effect. What could be simpler?

ANOTHER USE FOR WAX-BASED STAINS

If you should be lucky enough to own a paint sprayer, wax-based stain (in the darker colors) can be sprayed on a piece that has mixed woods you want to disguise. Don't wipe it off; just allow it to dry thoroughly, and then spray a clear finish over it. Of course, this covers and hides the grain, but at least you can get the right *color* over the entire piece with this method. This technique doesn't lend itself to brushing, however, as brushing produces streaks.

Finishes

There's a huge array of finishing products on the market, each claiming superiority over all the others. There are old-fashioned oil varnishes, polyurethane varnishes, water-based acrylic varnishes, shellac, lacquer, and tung oil, to name a few. It's understandable if you're confused.

If you're just starting out, you'd be wise to stick to one of a couple of finishes: water-based acrylic varnish or oil-based vinyl sealer/finish.

Water-Based Acrylic Varnish

You just can't beat acrylic varnish for most jobs. It dries fast, allowing you to apply several coats a day, and it rubs to a nice finish. Its only real disadvantage is that you can't apply it directly over a mahogany stain. If you've used a mahogany stain, you must coat the piece with an oil-based sealer or use the vinyl sealer and finish before applying acrylic varnish. The manufacturers warn you about this, too, so take our word on it and you'll avoid a sticky mess.

Oil-Based Vinyl Sealer and Finish

Unlike most other products discussed in this book, this wonderful product is made by only one manufacturer. It's called V. S. Vinyl Sealer and Finish, and it's available through the manufacturer, Reliable Finishing Products of Elk Grove, Illinois. (See the list of sources at the back of the book for details). It dries faster and can be sanded even sooner than the acrylic varnish; it also rubs to a nice finish. Because it's an oil varnish and sealer, it can be used over any type or color of stain. It thins and cleans up with paint thinner rather than water (unlike the acrylic product), but I can't think of any real disadvantages to this finish.

Applying Finish

The very best method for applying a finish to a piece of furniture is spraying. To do this properly, you have to invest thousands of dollars in sprayers, hoses, compressors, ventilators, and enclosures to trap the overspray. Few of us are willing to make such a commitment. The next best method to apply finish is a throwaway, foam rubber brush that costs less than a buck! I'm serious. Since the invention of these disposable tools, it's ridiculous to pay big money for imported, Chinese bristle brushes that need lots of care. When using either of the recommended finishes, the foam brush actually works better than the expensive brush alternative. Buy brushes that have wooden handles and dense foam if you can find them.

Before you tackle your first project, practice a little on a piece of scrap. You see, both of the recommended finishes don't take too well to being brushed over, once applied. If you try "brushing out" (i.e., the applying of pressure and repeated strokes of the brush), which is recommended for the application of slow-drying oil finishes, you're bound to mess up the surface.

Lay a good coat of finish on the piece, brushing (with the grain) in one direction and bringing the brush back over the same area only once. You need to work rather quickly, because it dries fast. Any imperfections in the stroke can be smoothed out in the sanding and rubbing stages.

Aerosols and Airbrushes

Because time is always a consideration, spray "turned" furniture legs rather than using a brush. Spraying allows for a nice even coat and covers hard-to-reach areas with ease.

Aerosols

Nowadays, you can get almost any kind of finishing material in an aerosol can. You might want to consider using a clear aerosol finish on the legs of a project. It'll speed that process up considerably, but you don't want to use it on an entire piece or on a tabletop. Believe me, these products were not designed for that use. Aside from the high cost, with aerosol paint it's nearly impossible to get a nice even finish on a large flat surface.

Airbrushes

Although I'm not an advocate of fancy gadgets, an airbrush is a worthwhile investment. It's like a miniature spray-painting outfit but uses a little ballpoint pen–sized sprayer instead of a big spray gun. An air brush is perfect for small projects such as frames, legs, pottery, and lamp bases; it's also handy for staining difficult areas.

Airbrushes themselves are pretty cheap, but the compressor that furnishes the air can be quite expensive. Fortunately, you don't need to buy a compressor. Instead, purchase cans of propellant to attach to the little airhose. Even if you do decide to buy a compressor, the total package will cost you considerably less than a "real" spray outfit and will quickly pay for itself in time savings.

Air from a Spare. All right, I'm feeling guilty about advising you to spend money on an airbrush — a genuinely nice-to-have tool — so I'm going to tell you how to save a little bit on the *air.* I was ashamed to mention it before, but those cans of propellant are pretty expensive! Instead of buying a compressor or propellant, go to a junkyard and get an old tire mounted on a wheel. It'll cost less than a can of "air," and with an adapter that you can get for the airbrush, it will furnish all the pressure you need. You can refill the tire again and again.

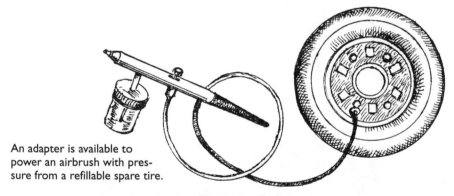

An adapter is available to power an airbrush with pressure from a refillable spare tire.

SPRAY LACQUERS

Colored spray lacquers are worth their weight in gold; unfortunately, that's the way they're priced, too. These lacquers come in a myriad of shades to match almost any wood or stain color. They're great for things like furniture legs and picture frames, and they add a nice touch when sprayed lightly over feather-painted or sponged surfaces. Because the lacquer is opaque, it enhances, rather than hides, whatever is under it. These lacquers can be difficult to find, so check the list of sources at the back of the book.

Between-Coat Sanding and Final Rubbing

The preparation, the between-coat sanding, and the final rubbing really determine how a piece will look when finished. If you neglect to do these properly, your finish will look lousy no matter what product you use or how you put it on.

Between Coats

Between coats of varnish, you must sand lightly. Use the fine wet-or-dry paper with a little water. Wipe it off occasionally with a damp rag, and check for smoothness.

Final Rubbing

After you've applied the last coat, which might be the second or third coat, do not sand. Using very fine (0000 grade) steel wool and a lubricant, rub the varnished surface down until it's velvety smooth to the touch. Rub *with* the grain. You can buy special rubbing lubricants, but I've found that a little diluted oil soap or some saddle soap works fine. If the surface needs a bit more leveling, common automobile rubbing compounds will do the trick. If you're happy with a "satin" sheen, you're finished. If you want a higher gloss, all you need to do is apply a coat of paste wax and buff. This simple step makes a huge difference in the quality of the finish.

What About the Legs?

It's difficult to do all that sanding and rubbing on spindles, carvings, and turned legs. Personally, I don't bother. Do make sure they're clean, wiping them with the tack rag between coats, but other than that, they don't need all the attention the flat surfaces get. Also, they usually don't require as many coats of finish.

THE TACK RAG

After the initial sanding, and especially after the sanding between coats, wipe your work off with a tack rag. A *tack rag* is a piece of cheesecloth impregnated with a sticky substance that picks up and holds any dust left from sanding. Tack rags don't cost much but can mean the difference between an amateurish job and a professional-looking finish.

Fast Finishes for Things Other Than Furniture

Please don't be one of those dealers who picks up a can of gold spray paint, shoots a coat on a picture frame, and hangs it in the shop. You know what that looks like? It looks like somebody just sprayed a coat of paint on a frame and stuck it in the shop. I'm sorry, but it's ugly! Here are a few simple techniques that take mere minutes to do but drastically alter the effect.

Highlighting

This finishing trick works on anything that's embossed or has a raised design, such as a mirror frame or the base of a bridge lamp. Using this technique, parts of the design are made to stand out from the background, thus highlighting these features.

> ┌── MATERIALS & TOOLS ─────────────────────
>
> - Airbrush or small, bristle   • Acrylic varnish
>   paintbrushes   • Rag
> - Water-based acrylic paint, two
>   colors (or one acrylic and
>   one aerosol)

1 Apply the background color and allow it to dry. You can use any color or type of paint, brushed or sprayed on by aerosol or airbrush. If you want it to look like aged brass or old gold leaf, buy brass-colored paint in an aerosol, not gold.

2 Mix a small amount of glaze, consisting of about half acrylic varnish and half acrylic paint. The paint color can be black, gray, reddish-brown, or any color you want to try.

3 Brush the glaze over the object being highlighted, getting it well into the recesses. If you're doing a large frame, do one side at a time, as the glaze dries rapidly.

4 Use a damp rag to remove most of the glaze from the raised portions of the design, leaving some in the recesses to "highlight" the piece.

Apply glaze.

Wipe glaze.

Faux Verdigris

Verdigris is the blue or green patina that forms naturally on copper, brass, or bronze that's been exposed to the elements, so this highlighting technique works especially well on metal.

MATERIALS & TOOLS

- Paintbrushes or airbrush
- Black gloss or semigloss paint (brush-on or aerosol)
- Blue and yellow acrylic craft paints

- Rag
- Clear finish

---

1 Paint the background black, using oil-based or water-based enamel, and allow to dry.

2 Mix blue and yellow acrylic craft paints together until you get a blue-green color resembling verdigris. (If you can't remember what verdigris looks like, leaf through a few magazines or decorator catalogs. It won't take you long to spot something done in this finish.) Brush the faux verdigris on, getting it well into the recesses.

3 Using a slightly damp rag, wipe the verdigris color off the edges and raised areas, exposing only a little black.

4 If the piece will be handled, once the paint dries you might want to coat the entire thing with a clear, low-gloss finish.

Wax-Based Rub-On Paints

If you don't want to mess with the highlighting techniques I've given you, at least go out and get a tube of rub-on paint and add a few interesting accents to your project. While I think any one of the other methods produces a better look, the rub-on-and-buff product will at least add some character, and make your piece unique.

▶ 10 ◀

trunk restoration
for the amateur

A nice, tastefully restored trunk is one item that even people who
don't ordinarily like antiques buy. Not only are they interesting accent
pieces, they provide extra storage space, something no one ever seems to
have enough of. Because trunk restoration is not beyond the abilities of
the average do-it-yourselfer, consider adding several to your inventory.

Some dealers think trunks should be taken as found; they'll even
tell you that complete renovation is a shame. Of course, these are the
dealers who have unrestored trunks in their shops. Consider it more like
refurbishing a Model-A Ford than a Louis XV armoire — this stuff was
once luggage, after all. Unlike furniture, I think you should buy trunks
with the sole intent of redoing them.

This chapter cannot possibly cover every eventuality. If you restore
trunks you'll have to contend with such things as trays and compartments that aren't addressed here. But once you've learned the basics,
you'll be able to improvise successfully in these situations.

Obviously, unlike most projects I encourage you to do, trunk restoration is no ten-minute task. It might even be a job you want to do a little
bit at a time. Like so many other things, the process is half the fun. Once
mastered, this could become yet another lucrative sideline for you.

Types and Styles of Trunks

In this chapter, I'll discuss five types and three styles of trunks. While
most of the restoration techniques are common to all trunks, others are
unique to a particular type or style. I'll explain the common procedures
without regard to the kind of trunk, supplementing that information
with the details necessary for you to tackle unique situations.

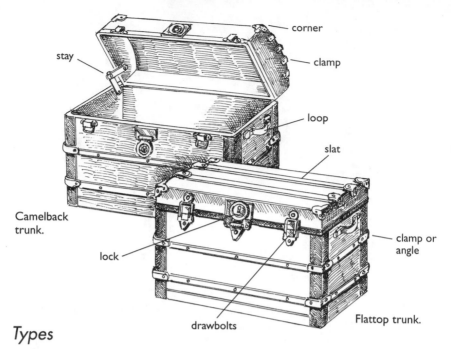

corner

stay

clamp

loop

slat

Camelback trunk.

lock

clamp or angle

drawbolts

Flattop trunk.

Types

By *type* of trunk, I mean the exterior covering. There are five: (1) smooth tin, (2) embossed tin, (3) canvas, (4) paper, and (5) leather.

Styles

The trunk's shape determines its *style*. The two most commonly restored styles are the *flattop*, which is basically a rectangular box, and the *camelback*, which has a rounded top. The latter style may also be referred to as a humpback, barrel-top, or oval-top trunk.

In addition to these, you might see large steamer trunks, bureau trunks with drawers, upright wardrobe trunks with built-in hangers, Jenny Lind styles with rounded tops and sides (which look sort of like a cross between a camelback and a flattop trunk), and toy or doll versions that duplicate the full-sized styles in miniature. Because the part names and the principles of restoration are essentially the same for all of these, I won't cover them in detail. Before attempting anything, study the illustrations of the two basic styles with their parts identified.

Restoring a Trunk

Trunk renovation is one of the jobs for which I've found relatively few shortcuts. It's also a task that requires a fairly extensive array of materials and tools. If you peruse the list that follows carefully, though, you'll see that with only a few exceptions they're things found even in a minimally equipped workshop. If this weren't such a rewarding undertaking, both personally and financially, I wouldn't include it in this book. Don't be overwhelmed! Just take it one step at a time. I've tried to make it easy for you by dividing it into four basic stages, with step-by-step directions for each stage.

MATERIALS & TOOLS

You won't need all these materials or every tool for every trunk you tackle. Some trunks will need relatively little work, while others will require extensive repair. This list covers everything you'll need for the worst-case scenario.

Materials

- Wood screws
- Saddle soap or oil soap
- Sandpaper
- White vinegar
- Wash-off stripping solution
- Hot water
- Wall "sizing" or wallpaper paste
- Epoxy putty
- Aluminum cans
- Carpet tacks
- Replacement parts (some you can make)
- New handles
- Trunk nails
- Corrugated cardboard
- Plywood, ½-inch thick
- Empty plastic bleach bottle
- Furniture glides
- Stain
- Flat black enamel
- Clear, satin finish
- Prepasted wallpaper
- Wood glue
- Leather (Don't ever throw away your old purses, wallets, or belts!)

Tools

- Screwdriver or tack remover
- End or side cutters (type of pliers)
- Hammer
- Blunt-end punch (about ⅛ inch)
- Steel wool, stripping pads, or stiff brush
- Rags
- Razor knife or single-edge razor blades
- Scraper
- Spray bottle
- Tin snips or heavy-duty scissors
- Flat piece of steel or an old flatiron
- Pop-rivet tool and rivets
- Jigsaw or coping saw
- Electric drill and soft wire brush for drill
- Foam brush and small 1-inch artist's brush
- Tape measure, pencil, and straightedge

Stage One: Removing Hardware/Interior Repairs

1 To begin removing the old handles, work the screwdriver or tack remover under the edges of the loops at the point where they're nailed. Exert gentle pressure to draw the nail out just far enough to get the jaws of the cutters under the heads. Cut off the nail heads. (These nails are curled into the wood on the inside, so pulling them all the way out might tear the wood, making it difficult to renail the replacement parts.) Don't worry if you break the loop — you can make a new one later. Follow the same procedure to remove the nails that go through the leather handles.

Draw the nail out enough so you can easily cut off the head.

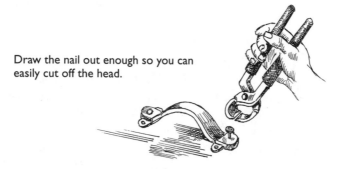

2 Tap the cut-off nails from the outside until you can see the curled ends emerge on the inside. (You might have to use the punch to drive them.) Use your cutters to grasp the nails and pull them out from the inside. If you can't seem to get these nails out, don't worry about it. Just cut the nails off flush with the surface. They'll be covered anyway.

Tap the nail through the wood and then pull it out from the inside.

3 Examine the bottom of the trunk. If even one of the castors is missing or broken, remove all four in the same manner as the handles.

4 Now begin to remove the stay, or lid support, just as you did the loops with one exception: Because the nails securing the stay were driven from the inside, they should simply be cut off flush on the inside. Don't try driving them out, as you'll damage the exterior of the trunk. Pay attention to how the stay was installed, because the little catch on it won't function if you reinstall it upside down. If you want, you can reattach the stay temporarily with wood screws so the lid won't flop around while you're working.

Don't try to remove a nail that holds the stay in place; just cut it off flush with the inside.

5 If a trunk is covered in leather or paper and the covering is in good condition, don't remove it, just clean it. Very fine steel wool with some saddle soap or oil soap usually will do the trick. If, on the other hand, the covering is in poor condition, or if the trunk is covered with canvas, remove it. Cut through the covering as close to the slats and hardware as you can get. A small razor knife works nicely. Be careful not to cut too deeply into the wood — it's usually pretty soft pine.

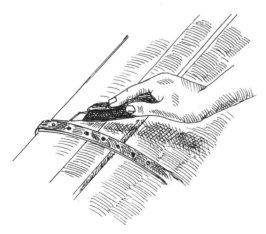

Cut completely through the old covering, keeping as close to the slats and hardware as possible and being careful not to damage the wood beneath.

6 If you're lucky the old covering will peel off, the glue having deteriorated over time. Usually you'll have to "encourage" the covering
off by scraping. This can be tough work, but the results are worth it.
Remove as much of the glue adhering to the wood as possible. A narrow,
sharp scraper, sandpaper, or a single-edge razor blade, used as a scraper,
might be needed to remove this residue. White vinegar, thoroughly
rinsed afterward, will sometimes help dissolve old glue.

Scrape off the old covering
and glue.

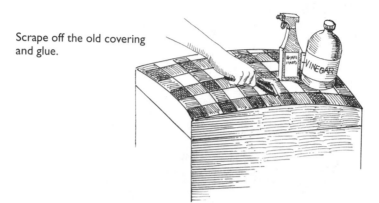

7 Strip the outside. You can treat the outside of the trunk like a piece
of furniture that you want to strip. (See chapter 8, pages 87–91, for
instructions.) Use liberal applications of wash-off stripper, stripping
pads, steel wool, and any other means necessary to remove the paint and
old finish. (It's easier to do the whole thing at once, rather than attempting to selectively strip some of it.) Hook a water hose to a hot water
source, spray the trunk down, and scrub the daylights out of it. It's best to
do this on a breezy or hot day, so the wood dries quickly. Don't forget to
turn the trunk over and do the bottom.

After coating liberally
with stripper, scrub
the entire trunk with
steel wool and hot
water.

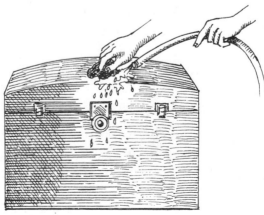

8 Remove the inside covering. Most trunks are covered on the inside with a rather thin paper. In most cases, this will have to be at least partially removed before re-covering. You'll find that if you've stripped the outside, some of the water and stripper will have worked itself inside and loosened some of the paper. Now you must remove as much of the remaining paper as you can. Scraping is the best method, and you can facilitate this process by keeping the paper damp as you work. Apply hot water with a spray bottle at regular intervals.

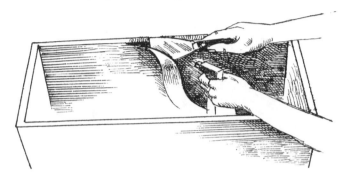

Remove as much of the old paper as possible.

9 Once you successfully remove all the old paper, brush on a coat of wall sizing or thinned wallpaper paste. This will seal the wood and allow for better adhesion of the new paper.

SIZING UP

Complete removal of the old interior covering usually works best, but here's a shortcut that you can use if the original paper is in pretty good shape: Brush a coat of wall sizing (available at paint and wallpaper stores in powdered or premixed form) or thinned wallpaper paste all over the inside. (This will seal the old paper and prevent it from coming loose when you repaper.) As it dries, you'll notice some bubbles and places where the old paper is lifting. Scrape just those spots and reprime with the sizing. Be sure to clean all the paper off the edges of the wood (where the lid and bottom come together).

Stage Two: Exterior Repairs

1 Repair damaged wood. Fill any holes in the exposed wood with a wood filler or epoxy putty. If you can get it, use an epoxy that's made for wood repair, as it will accept stain. This same material can be used to rebuild sections of wood that are broken or rotted. Don't forget to repair the bottom. It's not unusual for the slats on the bottom to be riddled with rot.

2 Repair tin. Holes or rusted-out areas of the tin sheeting that covers much of the trunk can be filled with the same epoxy material that you used for the wood. If there are areas too large to repair in this manner, *patches* can be made from pieces cut from an aluminum can. Just tack the patch to the body of the trunk using short carpet tacks. Don't even worry about the heads of the tacks or the edges of the patch being visible. Once you've painted everything, the patch will blend into the background.

Pieces of an aluminum can can be cut to size and used to patch rusted-out tin.

3 Replace missing parts. If the trunk you're restoring is missing its lock or any of the drawbolts, you'll have to purchase replacement parts from a supplier. (If you're not aware of any parts suppliers in your area, check the sources list at the back of the book.) At the very least, you'll need a source for new handles and trunk nails. Any of the other parts, such as the clamps, angles, castors, corners, and loops, can be substituted or easily made. (See the "Duplicating an Angle or Clamp" box for an example of how to do this.)

4 To attach a new angle or similar part to the wood of the trunk, drive a *trunk nail* through it and the wood. Since these special nails (which come in lengths from ½ inch to 1½ inches) are made to curl into the wood to hold fast, you have to hold a piece of steel on the inside

DUPLICATING AN ANGLE OR CLAMP

Cut a piece of corrugated cardboard larger than the piece you want to replicate, lay it against a good part, and tap it gently with a hammer. This will leave the outline of the part embedded in the cardboard, which you can then cut out and use as a pattern.

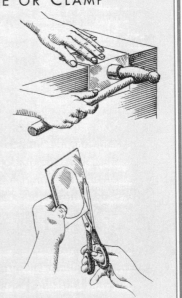

Double a piece of aluminum can by folding it as you would a piece of paper. Now, using your pattern, simply cut out the replacement part with a pair of sturdy shears or scissors, leaving the doubled metal attached along the seam.

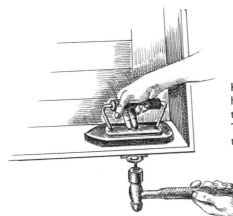

Hold an old flatiron or a piece of heavy steel on the inside of the trunk as nails are driven through. This bends and curls the point of the nail into the wood.

of the trunk, against the point, as you drive the nail from the outside. An old flatiron works nicely for this.

5 If you replace a latch or other part that was previously attached to the steel band that runs around the edge of the lid, use pop rivets to attach it.

6 If the castors on the bottom of the trunk need to be replaced, use
furniture glides, which are like big tacks with large polished steel or
plastic heads. They're made to be driven into the legs of tables and
chairs. Just drive them into the bottom of the trunk near the corners.

7 Although I don't cover it here, you'll find that on some trunks, various tabs and hinges on internal compartments were made of
leather. Your old purses and belts will serve as good sources for this
material, if any of these need to be replaced.

MAKING A SIMPLE PRESS

Automobile manufacturers use presses to form sheet steel into
autobody parts. In a few minutes, you can make a press that you can
use to form aluminum (cut from a soda or food container) into new
loops for covering the ends of the trunk handles. You can make other
parts using the same method, but I'll explain only the loops.

1. Cut two pieces of wood, 4 x 4", from a piece of ½" plywood. Using
   a jigsaw or coping saw, cut a notch in one piece that's as wide as
   the end of the new handle and about 1½" long. Use an old loop as
   a pattern if you have one. Save the piece (**a**) you cut out.
2. To make a hinge, cut a 4" strip of plastic from an old bleach bottle.
   Make it as wide as the two boards are
   thick. Attach your makeshift hinge to the
   top edge of the top board and to the
   bottom edge of the bottom board using
   carpet tacks.
3. Glue and nail piece **a** onto the bottom
   board, lining it up with the notch in the top.
4. Lay a piece of aluminum between the
   halves of the press, and step on the top
   board. When you remove the
   aluminum you will have the
   impressed shape of a handle
   loop. Trim the loop to the
   proper size with scissors.

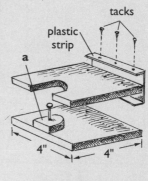

Stage Three: Finishing the Outside

1 With a soft wire brush chucked into an electric drill, run over all the metal, applying quite a bit of pressure to the straps, corners, latch, and any decorative features. Avoid hitting the adjacent wood, however. This brushing will brighten the hardware considerably, so you may choose not to paint it.

2 Sand and, if you wish, stain all the wood, but don't apply a finish yet. Remember to raise the lid and stain those edges. (See chapter 9, pages 93–101, for refinishing instructions.)

3 If you've replaced parts, you will have to paint them and probably all others so they match. Paint, but don't attach, the loops at the same time. If the trunk is totally covered in tin, paint it using two contrasting colors. Paint the tin that wraps around the corners and the outer edges with a flat black enamel, and paint the inner surfaces (those between the slats) with another color — personally, I like something subtle and subdued. You can use a foam brush to apply this paint, but you might have to resort to a small artist's brush to get close to the slats.

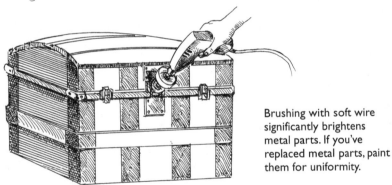

Brushing with soft wire significantly brightens metal parts. If you've replaced metal parts, paint them for uniformity.

4 Apply one or two coats of your favorite clear finish to the exterior surface of the trunk. This includes the tin, the wood (including the edges on the inside), and all the hardware.

5 Attach the handles and loops. Using the technique shown on page 113, drive long trunk nails through the handles, near the ends, curling the nails into the wood on the inside. Hold the loops over the ends of the handles, and drive shorter nails through the edges of the loops, also curling them inside. Touch up the loops with paint where you've marred them with the hammer.

Stage Four: Papering the Inside

1 Remove the temporarily attached stay, open the lid, and rest it on a padded surface. Then measure all interior dimensions (see illustration). Carefully note the width and the length for each dimension, writing down all of your measurements and labeling them. Don't shortchange yourself here, or you'll have to remeasure.

▸ Measure sides **A** and **B** and allow an extra 1 inch in the length and width of each side.
▸ Measure front **C** and back **D**. Allow an extra ½ inch in the width only.
▸ Measure bottom **E**. Do not allow for any extra.
▸ Measure top sides **F** and **G**. Allow an extra 1 inch in length and width. If it's a dome top, don't try to account for the curves in these pieces. Just measure as if the sides were rectangular.
▸ Measure top front and back **H** and **I**. Allow an extra ½ inch in width only.
▸ Measure top **J**. If a flattop, don't allow for any extra. If a dome top, use a flexible tape measure and follow the curve, then add at least 2 inches in width and length.

2 Measure, cut, and label all the wallpaper, envisioning where each piece will be placed. Keep the paper's pattern in mind. As when wallpapering a room, the design should not be upside down on one wall

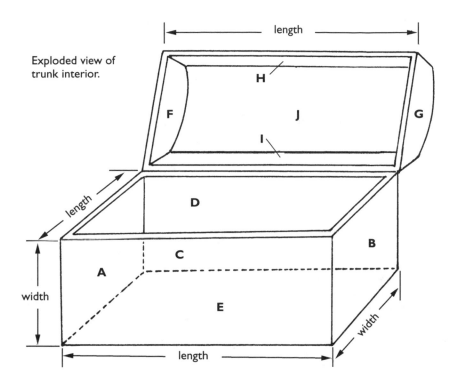

Exploded view of trunk interior.

length

H

F   J   G

I

length

D

B

C

A

width

E

width

length

(or side) and right side up on another. Pick a pattern that's appropriate for the trunk size, not something totally out of scale.

3 Soak the pieces for sides **A** and **B**, as prescribed for the prepasted paper. Place the paper against the side and slide it down until the top is even with the edge. Make sure the paper wraps around both corners and the bottom. Make a small slit where the bottom and sides meet, so the paper doesn't pucker in these corners. Smooth the paper by working the air bubbles out with a damp cloth or sponge. Don't be concerned about small bubbles, as they will disappear as the paper dries.

Make slits where paper bunches up in corners.

4 Repeat step 3 for pieces for sides **C** and **D**. These pieces will wrap onto the bottom, but just meet the corners to cover overlapped papers **A** and **B**.

5 Place section **E**, the bottom. If cut properly, this will just meet all the sides, covering the overlaps, but not extending up the sides.

6 Install sections **F** and **G** just as you did **A** and **B** (see step 3). If you're working on a dome top, there will be a lot of excess paper extending into the top, **J**. Don't trim it off, but make slits in it as shown. This will allow it to lie flat.

Make cuts wherever necessary to force paper to lie flat.

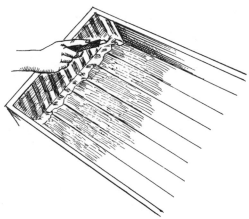

7 Cover **H** and **I** as you did **C** and **D**.

8 Install **J** in the same manner **E** was installed. If this is a dome top, it will be frustrating but not impossible to cover. In putting this paper in place, you'll have to make several long slits, running from the outside edges all the way to the center, to get it to lie flat against the wood. (Yes, it will throw off the symmetry of the pattern, but this can't be helped.) Where this paper meets the sides there will be overlap. Force it into the corners to crease the paper. Pull it back and trim these edges off along the creases.

tricks for cleaning silver and brass

I'm a cleaning fool! You wouldn't believe it if you saw my workshop or my office, but when it comes to the antiques I sell, I've found that clean ones sell better than dirty ones. In chapter 6, you learned my favorite tricks for cleaning wood furniture. Now I'm going to give you some help on difficult-to-clean silver, silver plate, and brass.

Silver and Silver Plate

Bright, lustrous silver adds class to any shop, while dull, tarnished items attract little attention and few buyers. Unfortunately, removing that black tarnish can be extremely difficult using traditional cleaning methods. There are a couple of quick methods to rid your pieces of tarnish, though: One uses muriatic acid, the other a professional dip.

Using Muriatic Acid to Clean Silver

I don't recommend this for Grandma's good silver or anything of great value, but the badly tarnished silver plate that you can pick up for next to nothing is worth buying if you can clean it almost instantly, which is what *muriatic acid* will do. Normally used for removing traces of mortar from brick, muriatic acid can be purchased at a hardware store. It is very corrosive, so treat it with respect. Wear acid-resistant gloves, and work outdoors or with plenty of ventilation.

MATERIALS & TOOLS

- Acid-resistant gloves
- Very fine (0000) steel wool
- Muriatic acid
- Silver polish

1 Set yourself up outside or in a well-ventilated area, and put on some acid-resistant gloves.

2 Dip a small amount of very fine steel wool in the acid and wipe, don't rub, the badly tarnished silver. Silver plating is microscopically thin, and vigorous rubbing will remove it completely.

3 If the area you're working on doesn't brighten immediately, allow the acid to work a few seconds and go back over it.

4 Rinse the item in plenty of water, and go over it with a little silver polish to give it some luster.

Cleaning Silver the Professional Way

Professionals use a "dip" to clean silver. For average levels of tarnish this method works well, and it's even less work than the acid method.

MATERIALS & TOOLS

- Two buckets or pots
- Aluminum foil
- Washing soda

- Hot water
- Detergent or dish soap
- Buffing cloth

1 Place a sheet of aluminum foil in the bottom of a large container, such as a 5-gallon bucket or a big stainless steel soup pot, and lay the item you want to clean on top of the foil.

2 In a separate container, mix a solution of common washing soda (available in the detergent section of the grocery store) at the rate of 1 cup to 1 gallon of hot water. The water should be as hot as you can get it from the tap, not boiling. Mix enough to totally cover the tarnished object.

3 Pour the hot washing soda over the item until it's completely immersed.

4 Within a half hour, retrieve the item from the container and rinse the tarnish away in warm, sudsy water.

5 Dry, and buff with a soft cloth.

Silver can be dipped in a washing soda solution.

Brass

You've got some brass, and it's dark and dull, not all that appealing. Brightly polished brass, on the other hand, glitters and reflects light. In some way, be it heft or color, brightly polished brass resembles gold, and people prefer to buy brass objects in that state. Getting it to and maintaining that condition can be quite labor-intensive, however, so some quick cleaning tricks are in order. We'll begin with suggestions for stripping lacquer away from brass.

Stripping Lacquer from Brass

Most of us, at one time or another, have gotten hold of a piece of tarnished brass and attempted to clean it with brass polish and a rag. No matter how hard we rubbed, we didn't accomplish much. Why? Because most brass objects are lacquered to prevent corrosion. Over the years, persistent, corrosive little molecules of oxygen break through the lacquer and darken the brass. So in order to polish it, you must first remove the lacquer. For larger objects — anything from a brass bed to a lamp — I recommend treating it just as you would a piece of furniture.

MATERIALS & TOOLS

- Paintbrush
- Paint remover

- Medium steel wool
- Water (or lacquer/paint thinner)

---

1 Brush on a generous coat of paint remover and allow it to work for about 5 minutes. Keep the piece wet, as you would when stripping a coat of paint from a piece of wood furniture. Note that the thin coating of lacquer on a piece of brass usually dissolves a lot faster than do finishes on furniture.

2 Using *medium* steel wool, scour the item and then wash it off if you're using a water-soluble stripper, or clean it with lacquer/paint thinner and steel wool.

Cleaning the Bare Brass

After you've removed the lacquer from the surface of brass, you still don't have something that's shiny and bright. Normally, at this point, the oxidized surface that was beneath the lacquer requires additional cleaning and polishing to brighten it. There's no need to struggle with this step, either. You have several options: muriatic acid, ammonia, or hard water stain remover.

Muriatic Acid. Our friend is back again, this time to brighten discolored brass. Use the muriatic acid *exactly* as previously prescribed for the removal of tarnish on silver (see page 120). If the brass is not too oxidized, you might get away with diluting the acid with 50 percent water. Pour the acid *into* the water, not vice versa, to avoid splashing the stronger of the two onto your skin. Follow this treatment by rinsing the piece with plenty of water.

Ammonia. This is the cheapest and one of the most effective agents for cleaning brass. If the piece is only moderately tarnished, you can just wet a piece of steel wool with ammonia and rub the brass vigorously. It won't work instantly, like the muriatic acid, but it works quickly enough and with very little effort. Alternatively, pour a few gallons of ammonia into a large container; wrap a wire around the item, leaving one end out

BOIL AND BUBBLE, NO TOIL AND TROUBLE

Here's the fastest way I know to remove lacquer from small brass items:

Into a pot no more than half-full of water, add about 3 tablespoons of washing soda per quart of water. (Common baking soda also works, but double the amount.) Place the small tarnished objects in the pot and bring to a boil. You'll see why the pot is only half-full, when a dirty foam begins to form. The dirt in the foam is the dissolving lacquer. Trust me, you don't want this stuff boiling over on your stove, and you don't want to use the good cookware, either. (My wife emphatically pointed that out to me once.) This is a practical use for some of those pots and pans no one else wants to buy at an auction.

After the object has boiled for anywhere from 5 to 30 minutes, pour off the liquid and go over the piece with steel wool to loosen any remaining flakes. Voilà!

of the container for easy removal; and soak the brass item for several hours if badly tarnished or for several minutes if not so bad. Remove from the soak, and brighten with steel wool. (Be sure not to stick an ungloved hand in there. The soak won't harm you, but your skin will be green for at least a week — another lesson I learned the hard way.)

Hard Water Stain Remover. My wife and I live in a rural area, and our water supply is a well. It's good water but extremely hard (that is, it has a lot of dissolved limestone and other minerals in it.) Because of this, we always have some hard water stain remover around. This is the stuff that's supposed to remove lime scale and soap scum, caused by hard water.

Soaking brass in ammonia will help clean it, but only if the lacquer has already been removed.

On one occasion, when I was cleaning up an old oil lamp, I found that I was out of muriatic acid and ammonia. I didn't feel like running to the store, so I looked around for a substitute. On a hunch, I tried a little of the lime remover and was pleased to discover that the acids in that product were quite effective in removing tarnish from brass. Use it with steel wool and rub vigorously. Follow by rinsing in water.

Hand Polishing Brass

After you've removed the lacquer and tarnish from brass, the surface has been etched dulled) by the cleaning process, and polishing to a brilliant shine becomes easy. You can obtain a brilliant shine by using very fine (0000) grade steel wool and a paste type of metal polish. Liquid brass polishes work, but I like the kind that comes in a tube and has the consistency of toothpaste.

The paste polish has several advantages, including its oily base, which provides more lubrication. This allows you to achieve a greater luster and also slows the drying process, which extends the working time for a single application. That, in turn, translates to slightly less product used. The slower drying also gives you time to buff off the residue with a rag, and doesn't leave ugly white powder in the crevices.

Polishing the Professional Way

Hand polishing works fine, but if you really want a professional look, try a buffing machine. You know I'm no big spender, and I won't tell you to buy something unless I think it will pay for itself over time. An electric buffing machine is worth the small investment, but remember to keep it simple and cheap! Don't rush out and buy a machine designed specifically for buffing. They're available, but unless you're going to polish metals only, their cost is prohibitive. Instead, buy a small bench-mounted grinder. You can find them at mail-order houses or at the local home supply center. One-quarter horsepower is sufficient.

In addition, buy three spiral-stitched muslin buffing wheels with holes the same size as the shafts of the motor. These wheels are usually a little larger than the grinding wheels that come with the motor, so you might have to remove the guards that partially cover the wheels — they won't serve any purpose on a buffer, anyway. (The guards are there to protect your hands from the sharp edges of the grinding wheel and to deflect particles of metal or wheel from being thrown at your eyes.) At the same time, get a soft or medium wire wheel that will fit the same shaft size.

A buffing wheel and buffing compound quickly brighten brass pieces.

Replace the grinding wheels with the muslin wheels on one shaft and the wire wheel on the other. You'll find a million uses for the wire wheel, from removing final traces of lacquer from the items you intend to buff, to removing rust and paint from other small objects. Be sure to replace the guard on the wire wheel side before use.

You'll need some buffing compound, too. It comes in various grades and types, but you can make out nicely with jeweler's rouge. (If you can't find it, check the source list at the back of the book.) Jeweler's rouge comes in a solid stick and is applied to the moving wheel, after which it is allowed to dry for a few seconds. Put on your safety glasses and gloves, then hold the object you want to polish against the surface of the wheel. Don't apply much pressure — let the fine abrasives in the buffing compound do the work. Very quickly you'll produce a finish comparable to that of a fine piece of jewelry.

Lacquering

After polishing brass, you need to protect it from rapid oxidation. A coat of any good paste wax will slow the darkening, but not for long. The longest-lasting protection is obtained by applying a coat of gloss lacquer. Before you lacquer, be sure you thoroughly remove any traces of buffing compound by wiping the object with a clean rag and inspecting it closely. (If you can't find lacquer in aerosol cans locally, see the source list at the back of the book.)

Darkening Brass

In addition to knowing how to clean and polish brass, you need to know how to darken it. There will be a few occasions when it's necessary to make a brass item look older than it is — when replacing a single drawer pull, for instance.

I imagine by now you know how much I relish finding home remedies for problems related to the restoration of antiques. Sometimes, though, I must concede defeat. Such is the case with my search for a homemade agent for darkening brass and copper — I gave up long ago. The only formulas I could find used chemicals like potassium polysulfide or iron chloride, which are difficult to obtain. To darken brass, purchase a "patinizing" solution at an art supply dealer. (If you can't find it, check the list of sources at the back of the book.)

If you want to try a cheap do-it-yourself method, there is one solution that you can mix at home, but frankly, I'm not sure it's worth the trouble. Whichever method you use, you should protect the finish with a coat of wax or lacquer after achieving the desired degree of darkening.

Pickling. Yes, literally pickle the brass. This is an old trick for "growing" a patina, or accelerating a verdigris finish on brass, copper, or bronze. After cleaning the brass and abrading the surface with fine steel wool, brush on or dip the piece in a solution of vinegar and salt. Old dill pickle juice will do. After wetting, allow it to sit for an hour, then repeat the process until you've achieved the color you want. It works, but usually produces a mottled appearance. Unless you want it, remove the green tinge that collects in some areas. This process can take many applications.

fixing

If it ain't broke, don't buy it! Good advice, but don't take me too literally here. After all, if you bought nothing but broken and damaged antiques and collectibles, you'd spend all your time repairing them. And that certainly wouldn't leave much time for seeking out other bargains. The fact remains that the more repair work you are willing to do, typically the less money you have to spend, which translates into higher profits. Even if you don't seek out these types of purchases, you'll occasionally need to make a repair or will feel compelled to salvage something just a little too good to throw away.

In the next few chapters, you'll receive direction on repairing pottery and ceramics; re-covering lampshades without sewing a stitch; renovating, repairing, and converting lamps and lighting; resurrecting frames; performing tricks with mirrors; and making common furniture repairs.

As usual, doing the job quickly, easily, and cheaply without sacrificing quality is emphasized.

▸12◂

mending chipped and broken pottery

American art pottery has steadily escalated in value over the years, and many pieces that were mass-produced and sold inexpensively in dime stores now command shockingly high prices. You'll recall that I talked about the "Big Four" of Roseville, Weller, Hull, and McCoy in chapter 4, and that I advised you to buy any one of these, even if it's slightly damaged and cheap. That advice still stands.

Some years ago I bought an unusual Roseville jardiniere at an auction. It was in a box lot, and apparently no one else recognized it. I could hardly believe it when I got this precious piece for almost nothing.

My joy was short-lived, however, as a couple of weeks later I bumped it off a fern stand and knocked a big chunk out of it. My wife had just turned down a nice offer for it, so needless to say, we were both in shock. My carelessness had cost us the possibility of a handsome profit, not to mention the fact that a thing of beauty seemed lost. There was no need for discussion: This piece had to be repaired. We packed it up and hurried to a nearby repair shop.

The repair, although very costly, was quite noticeable. Then and there I decided that I could do at least as good a job. That was the beginning of a long process of trial and error that eventually resulted in techniques that I'm going to share with you now.

I've been told more than once that this type of work, "ceramics conservation," should be attempted only by those with fine sensibilities and lengthy artistic training. To them I say, "Gimme that pot! I'll fix it!" Armed with just rudimentary knowledge and simple tools, any of us can do this job.

How to Mend Pottery

Mending a piece of damaged pottery or any other ceramic item requires removal of any old repairs, rough filling, leveling, final filling, and smoothing the new repair. After that, you still need to restore the coloring and coat the piece, both of which I'll discuss later. For now, let's stick to the actual mending.

MATERIALS & TOOLS

- Small knife or other pointed instrument
- Water
- Acetone (nail polish remover)
- Lacquer thinner
- Single-edge razor blades
- Epoxy putty

- Small, fine file or 1-inch wood sanding block
- Medium and fine wet-and-dry sandpaper
- Stiff cardboard or foam brush insert
- Automobile glazing or spot putty

---

1 The most common repair you'll do is the replacement of chips or "flakes." Often you'll get a piece that has been glued together, with the broken fragment shard stuck back in place. I recommend removing it and throwing it away. You might be reluctant to do this, thinking you should preserve every tiny fragment. If it's a priceless museum piece, that's probably true, but you really shouldn't be working on those.

First, try prying the piece out. Get under an edge with the blade of a knife or another sharp, pointed instrument, and try to dig it out. If a household cement was used to make the repair, chances are the fragment will pop right out. Don't be afraid to break the small piece — you're going to discard it anyway.

If it won't come out easily, try soaking the piece overnight in water. If that doesn't loosen it, try acetone (nail polish remover), which dissolves most common glues.

If a piece has been glued on, it's best to remove it and start over.

Lacquer thinner should be your last resort. If none of the solvents work, you'll be forced to carefully *chisel* the old repair out — fortunately that almost never happens. After the chip is removed, use a razor blade to scrape the surface free of any remaining glue, and wash the damaged area with soap and water.

2 Mix a small amount of the epoxy putty. Prepare just a little more than necessary to fill in the space that's missing. Force the putty into the space, allowing it to overhang the damaged area slightly. Don't try to achieve a smooth, contoured, finished surface at this step. Allow the epoxy to cure.

3 With a small file or a tiny sanding block made with a 1- × 1-inch scrap of wood and medium sandpaper, level the repair with the surrounding surface. Be careful! You don't want to badly scratch the glaze surrounding the repair; some minor scratching is unavoidable. Again, don't try to get the filling perfectly smooth at this time.

4 Using either a piece of stiff cardboard with a straight edge or the plastic insert removed from the inside of a disposable foam brush, apply a thin coat of the automobile glazing or spot putty. Allow it to dry for about 30 minutes.

Step 3: Fill with epoxy putty, then sand.

Step 4: Apply spot putty.

5 Cut a very small square of the fine wet-and-dry sandpaper and, holding it on the tip of your finger, sand the patch, keeping the surface wet. Check to be sure the repaired area is perfectly even with the surrounding surface. If you can feel a transition — either slightly higher or lower — when you run your fingertips over the area of the repair, you need to sand more or repeat step 4.

Coloring

Coloring is the most difficult task in restoring ceramics. I would love to give you some simple, foolproof methods for this step, but the best I can do is steer you in the right direction and give you some hard-earned tips.

Every piece of pottery is unique and must be approached differently. Although a piece may have been mass-produced, different people applied the glazes on different days, in different ways, and in different years. The temperature of the kilns might have varied slightly, and two seemingly identical pieces may not have spent the same amount of time being fired. When you begin mixing colors, there are no exact formulas, only general recommendations.

TWO KEY DISCOVERIES

Two things that art majors learn on the first day of class (if they don't instinctively know it) took me ages to discover through experimentation:

1. **An object created with the intent of pleasing the eye is rarely just one color, even though, without close scrutiny, it appears to be so.** Sounds simple? It is simple, but beginning restorers drive themselves nuts trying to match a single hue when in fact it can never be matched because it's really two, three, or more colors, not blended together, but intermingled and sometimes layered, one atop the other.

   Try this experiment: Look at something in the room you're in right now. Maybe that brick in the fireplace. Quick! What color is it? Brown? Look again, but more closely. It's brown *and* white and red and gray and yellow.

2. **Lighting makes all the difference.** The first piece of pottery I restored changed color magically as I was carrying it from the house to the car. Suddenly I saw the light, literally and figuratively. Work with as much natural light as possible. Also, keep in mind that the same color will look different in incandescent light and with fluorescent lighting. Don't be satisfied with a color match until you've taken it outside.

Your Paints

Use only acrylics. Some you can buy in little bottles at craft stores; some you'll need to buy in tubes of artist's colors. Since there is an infinite array of colors to choose from, start with the basics. Buy colors that are as dark and pure as possible. Don't buy "appleberry–plum pudding–Christmas morning" red. These ten colors will provide you with a surprising range of hues: (1) black, (2) white, (3) yellow ochre, (4) raw sienna, (5) burnt sienna, (6) raw umber, (7) burnt umber, (8) red, (9) yellow, and (10) blue.

In addition, you'll need clear, acrylic varnish, which is also available in small craft-sized bottles. After you've gained some experience and confidence mixing colors, add some other colors to your palette, such as phthalo blue or shiva green.

A Remedial Class in Color Mixing

Most of us learned how to make different colors when we were in elementary school, but time often robs us of such early memories. Here's a refresher:

Blue + yellow = green
Red + yellow = orange
Blue + red = purple
Red + yellow + blue + black = brown

Adding white changes the tint of a color (makes it lighter), while adding black alters the shade (black absorbs less light, making the color appear darker).

Those are the basics, but it's impossible to equip you with all the subtleties. It's easy to see how varying amounts of blue can change a color from green to blue-green or chartreuse, or shift purple toward or away from violet — the possibilities are limitless. Experience is often our greatest teacher, so have fun and experiment.

Here are a few less obvious combinations to get you started:

Orange + raw sienna = rust
Orange + burnt umber = a darker rust
Burnt-umber rust + red = plum
Plum + a touch of black = burgundy
Green + raw sienna = olive
White + yellow ochre = ivory
White + raw sienna = cream

SOME ADDITIONAL PAINTING POINTERS

▸ A white ceramic glaze can be the most difficult to make. Many shades of white can be duplicated by adding to white a tiny trace of one of the following: raw sienna, raw umber, or, surprisingly, blue.

▸ When you've mixed the color and it's close but just not quite right, add a tad of yellow ochre or raw sienna. Many of the colors used by the makers of the more popular art pottery lines have a tinge of one of those colors, especially those that you might think are pink.

▸ When you can't seem to find the right shade of blue, it might be because it's deep purple. Add some red. If it's not dark enough, add black.

▸ When mixing colors, a white Styrofoam plate makes the best palette. The pure white background provides an excellent contrast to any color you put on it. Since they're cheap and disposable, you don't waste time cleaning them, either. Don't try using paper plates: Tiny, hairlike fibers are apt to come off the paper and end up in your paint.

▸ If paint isn't dry, you don't know its true color. Remember when you blend colors that acrylic paints dry darker than they appear when wet. Put a touch of paint on the item at a place other than your repair, and dry with a hair dryer to check the match. Naturally, you'll wipe these experiments off. A damp cloth easily removes them.

▸ The brown "drip" glazes popular on a lot of early stoneware can be duplicated by mixing water-soluble aniline stains or furniture "powders" with acrylic varnish. (See the source list at the back of the book for more information.)

Painting and Finishing Pottery

Once you're satisfied with the color you've mixed, the best applicator, in most cases, is the tip of your finger covered by a piece of linen. A good soft-bristled artist's brush will work on some repairs, but they tend to leave brush marks. Although it's not essential, one of those small airbrushes that I talked about in chapter 9, can be really handy when working on something like a solid-color pastel Hull piece.

MATERIALS & TOOLS

- Styrofoam plates
- Old linen handkerchief, napkin, or other tightly woven cloth
- Selection of acrylic paints and acrylic varnish
- Small artist's brushes

- Optional items
  Small airbrush
  Soft lead pencil
  Lacquer in aerosol cans
  Fine steel wool
  Paste wax

---

1 Mix your paint on your Styrofoam palette.

2 Get a little of your mixed paint on the cloth and gently pat it onto the repair. Don't apply it to the repair only; rather, "blend" the repair into its surroundings by applying the paint very lightly to the area adjacent to the patch.

CRAZING

The pattern of fine, sometimes barely discernible, lines in the glaze on some pottery is called *crazing*. If the surface you repair is crazed, a sharp soft lead (such as a 2B) pencil can be used to lightly draw in some craze lines over the finished paint before the final coating is applied.

---

3 If there's more than one color present, apply the base color first. Then mix your next color and dilute it with a little clear varnish. Dab this over the base color. It's possible that you'll need to do this with several colors to achieve the right effect.

Pat color on.

4 When your repair has been painted, protect it with a clear finish. Always give your work a coat of acrylic varnish. It comes in an exterior grade that is a little tougher than regular. The exterior grade is preferable but not a necessity.

5 You could stop at step 3, but I recommend topping the whole thing with one or two layers of an aerosol lacquer. If you plan to apply lacquer, you must use the acrylic varnish first. The lacquer alone, over some acrylics, intensifies the colors.

6 The finish can be adjusted from glossy to satin to matte with very fine (0000) steel wool, used with or without paste wax.

FOOT REPAIRS

If your repair involves the bottom (or foot) of the pot, it's usually not glazed. Paint it (usually a shade of cream or ivory) and rub a piece of newspaper over the paint after it dries. The ink will come off in irregular streaks, blending the repair into the rest of the bottom.

---

no-sew lampshade
re-covering

Lampshades are very expensive. Even at wholesale prices, they can sometimes be more costly than the lamps for which they're intended. It just isn't practical to put a thirty-dollar shade on a lamp that you've purchased for five bucks. There are obvious exceptions to this, of course. Some lamps that you acquire at a bargain price cry out for an exquisite shade — we'll talk about those in the next chapter. Almost any shade is better than no shade at all when you display a lamp for sale. What we need to do is concentrate on creating an attractive shade for an average lamp.

By doing it yourself you can resell the lamp quickly at a low price and still make a profit. A competitor selling a comparable lamp, equipped with even a cheap off-the-shelf shade, must ask a much higher price to recoup the investment.

Old, disheveled lampshades are certainly not hard to come by. You can pick them out of the piles of discards at auctions, friends will save them for you, or you might find a few on trash-collection days.

THE CALENDAR SHADE

Have you been saving attractive calendars, thinking someday you might frame the prints. Well, here's another use for them. When replacing the cover on a flat-sided, hexagonal shade, cut the sections out of the prints of one of the calendars. Each panel will be complementary and unique. Of course, the look of this type of shade really depends on your taste in calendars.

Re-covering Lampshades

Not every old shade will do for re-covering. You want either of the following: (1) a straight-sided hexagonal (or other sectional) shade; or (2) a shade that has no ribs, only a top and bottom ring, or a shade with straight, not bowed-in, ribs connecting the top and bottom rings. Repair procedures for these two types of shade differ somewhat. We'll begin with a hexagonal shade and then move on to one with circular rings.

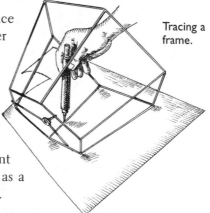

MATERIALS & TOOLS

- Old shade frame
- Poster board or other stiff paper
- Pencil
- Two 1-pound bags of dried beans

- Sharp scissors
- Glue
- Wooden, spring-type clothespins
- Single-edge razor blades
- Crayon or colored chalk
- Glue applicator (optional)

Hexagonal Shade

1 To remove the covering from a hexagonal shade, cut and rip it off in any manner, but don't bend the frame.

2 To mark the new cover, place the frame on a sheet of poster board or other stiff paper, and use your pencil to trace around the outside of one of the sections.

Tracing a frame.

3 Cut out the section, staying outside the marks to allow a little room for adjustment later on. Use the cutout section as a pattern to make the other sections.

4 To attach the first section of the new cover, run a bead of glue along the outside of one section of the frame first. (Use a thick, craft glue that will stick to metal and paper.) Attach the paper to the frame with

spring-type clothespins around all four edges. Let the glue dry, or accelerate the drying with a hair dryer. Trim any overlap of the paper with a sharp razor blade.

5 Attach other sections in the same manner, using clothespins to secure three edges. The fourth edge of the section is held against the frame by the weight of a bag or two of beans. The final section is clipped at the top and bottom and weighted on each side.

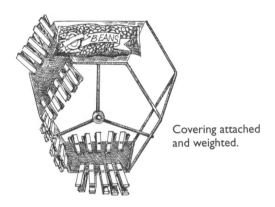

Covering attached
and weighted.

Shade with Circular Rings

1 To remove an old fabric covering, cut and rip it off in any manner possible without bending the frame. If the frame is covered with paper, parchment, or plastic, a gentler approach is necessary in order to preserve the old cover for use as a pattern. Use a razor blade to cut the trim that covers the rings. Next, carefully insert the blade under the edge of the seam that joins the ends of the covering, and work this glued seam loose. You might have to work from both the inside and the outside. At this point the entire covering should come off the frame, and you will be holding an arc-shaped piece of material. Use the scissors to tidy the ragged edges.

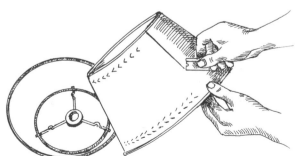

A single-edge razor
blade is used to cut
old paper cover away
from frame.

2 *If you're working from an arc,* mark the new cover by laying the old one on a sheet of poster board or other stiff paper and trace around it.

If you don't have an arc pattern to work from and the frame is a one piece (not two unattached rings), rub a little crayon or colored chalk on the outer edges of the rings and roll the frame on the paper. This will mark a pattern.

Trace an arc.

3 Cut the marked paper, staying slightly outside the marks to allow for adjustment later on.

4 Starting with the top ring, attach the paper with a spring-type clothespin. Continue all the way around the ring, placing the clothespins side by side. Repeat for the bottom ring. You might have to loosen pins here and there to adjust the fit as you go. The cover should fit snugly to the frame.

Attach new covering.

5 Once attached, glue the covering to the frame. To do this, remove every other clothespin from the top ring. Then, with the bottle of glue or a glue applicator (simply a bottle with a long thin nozzle), reach inside the shade and apply a bead of glue along the paper where it touches the frame. This will "tack" the paper to the frame. (If you can't locate a glue applicator at your local craft store, consult the source list at the back of the book.)

Glue the arc.

6 Repeat this process for the bottom ring and for any inside ribs. When the glue dries, remove all the clothespins and apply glue to the spaces that were covered by the pins.

7 There should be about a ½-inch overlap where the two ends of the arc come together. Using your finger or a piece of stiff paper, coat the underside of the overlapping edge with a little glue (too much glue will squeeze out from under the paper onto the outside). Lay the shade on its side, seam down on a clean surface, and place a bag or two of beans inside the shade. The weight will press the surfaces together. Leave the beans in place until the adhesive sets and the seam is sealed.

Decorating the Shade

If you've used an attractive, textured paper to cover your shade, you need do nothing else — you have a simple, completed shade. If you used poster board, you can paint it with an aerosol paint or even marbleize or sponge paint it (see chapter 7 for details).

For a more elegant look *before* it's attached to the frame, spray the paper with adhesive that comes in a pressurized can, or paint it with some glue diluted with water. Next, place a piece of fabric flat on your work surface, wrong side facing, and press the now sticky paper onto the fabric. Trim the edges with scissors.

A Finishing Touch

It's not absolutely necessary, but you might want to cover the edges of the shade at the top and bottom rings. For this, you'll need ribbon that is at least 50 percent cotton; otherwise, the glue won't adhere to it. The type of ribbon most commonly used is a ribbed variety called grosgrain ("grow grain"). (If you're unable to find the ribbon or are interested in other shade supplies, see the source list at the back of the book.)

Measure around the shade at top and bottom, and cut the ribbon to that length, allowing a little extra to overlap. Apply the glue to the ribbon and wrap the glue-covered portion over the wire, pressing it against the paper on the inside and outside of the shade. Work on sections of about 1½ inches at a time, and use a clothespin to hold the ribbon in place temporarily as you work on the next section. When you reach the end, just overlap it, glue, and clamp it into place.

renovating and converting lamps

Unique and attractive floor and table lamps are constantly sought by interior decorators and homeowners. Although they're a staple in many antiques shops, some dealers avoid buying them if they're not in good working order. If dealers do purchase them, they either attempt to sell them "as is" (limiting the potential market), or they pay someone like me to rewire or repair them.

There's really nothing mysterious or dangerous about doing these things yourself, and learning the basics of these simple tasks will give you yet another advantage over some dealers. I can't prepare you for every situation you'll encounter, of course, but this chapter will get you through about 90 percent of the repairs you'll need to make and teach you a few tricks for converting lamps.

Reviving a Table Lamp

If a lamp doesn't work, the problem can only be in one of three places: the plug, the cord, or the socket. Unless the lamp is rather new, you might as well replace all three while you're at it. Before you start, however, study the illustration on page 143 to familiarize yourself with lamp terminology.

┌─ MATERIALS & TOOLS ──────────────────────

- Screwdriver
- Electrical cord
- Sharp knife or single-edge razor blade
- Wire stripper

- Socket interior
- Automatic plug
- Replacement felt
- Craft glue
- Scissors

└──

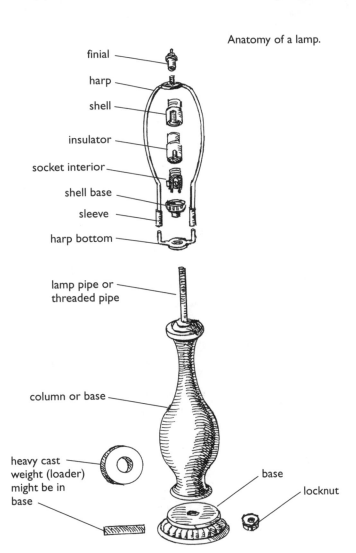

Anatomy of a lamp.

finial

harp

shell

insulator

socket interior

shell base

sleeve

harp bottom

lamp pipe or
threaded pipe

column or base

heavy cast
weight (loader)
might be in
base

base

locknut

1 Remove the harp — it's easier to take the shell off the socket if the harp is out of the way first. With the lamp unplugged, lift the two little sleeves where the top attaches to the bottom of the harp. Squeeze the sides of the harp near this attachment and remove the top part.

2 Take the socket apart. Look at the socket where the shell meets the cap. You'll see the word *press* near the switch opening. Push in on this with your thumb and tilt the shell toward the opposite side. The shell will come off, exposing the socket. If you're unable to loosen the shell, insert a small screwdriver at the "press" point. This will usually dislodge it.

3 Disconnect the old wire. When you remove the shell, the cardboard insulator usually remains in it. If it's still covering the socket, pull it off. Loosen the two screws that hold the lamp cord to the socket, and pull the cord out from the bottom of the lamp. You might have to take the felt off the base of the lamp to access the cord.

4 Feed the new cord, which should be 6 to 8 feet long, through the base and up through the lamp pipe and socket cap. Allow yourself plenty of slack at the top and tie a loose, ordinary knot in the cord several inches from the end. With a sharp knife or razor blade, slit the insulation between the two wires, just enough to start the separation. Pull the two wires apart a couple of inches, and strip about a ½ inch of insulation off each wire. Roll the wire between your thumb and index finger to twist all those little fine wires together.

5 *If you're using a polarized cord and plug* (one prong wider than the other), you'll note that one wire is copper colored and the other is silver. Just match the wire colors to the colors of the screws on the socket. What this does is place the grounded side of the circuit on the threaded, outer portion of the socket — the part you could most easily touch by accident. I won't give you a course in electricity here, but this arrangement is a precaution to prevent shocks.

If the cord doesn't have two different colored wires or if the plug isn't polarized, you can place the wire under either screw. (Note that you don't have to buy an entire socket — shell, insulator, and cap. You can buy just the electrical part; it's cheaper.)

6 Making sure there are no stray strands of wire, tighten the screws securely. Work the loose knot up as close to the bottom of the interior as possible, pull the slack out of the cord from the bottom, and replace the shell and insulator. You'll feel it snap into place as you push the shell into the cap.

Wiring socket with knot.

7 Replace the plug. I see no reason to use old-fashioned screw-type plugs when rewiring lamps. Instead, use an automatic plug. To attach one, squeeze the prongs together and pull the insides out. Insert the end of the cord through the hole in the cover and, holding the prongs spread outward, force the cord as far as possible into the opening between the prongs. Squeeze the prongs together and push the mechanism back into the cover, seating it firmly.

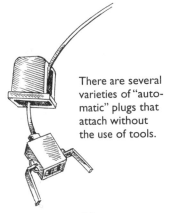

There are several varieties of "automatic" plugs that attach without the use of tools.

If the plug has one prong wider than the other and the cord has a silver and copper-colored wire, the silver side goes to the wide prong. Don't be concerned if the lamp cord or the plug is not polarized. Most aren't and, believe me, you aren't going to electrocute anyone. There's no backward way to wire a single-socket lamp!

8 Replace the felt. Normally, you'll destroy the felt on the bottom of a lamp when you rewire it. You can buy replacement felt from parts suppliers (even self-stick) or, for a lot less money, in small sheets at craft stores. Use a thick craft glue. Spread a coat on the base and set the lamp on top of the felt. After the glue has dried, trim the excess close to the base with sharp scissors.

ARMS AND HEADS

Am I about to describe a scene from a horror movie? No, but rewiring the arms of a lamp or chandelier, or some bridge lamp heads, can be a horrifying experience unless you use the bead-chain trick.

Once you've pulled the old wire out of one of these things, you can find it next to impossible to snake in new wire. Instead of trying to push the wire through, drop one end of a strong bead chain into one end of the arm, and tilt the arm. Gravity will encourage the chain to come out the other end. Wrap the stripped ends of the new wire around several of the beads, and pull the chain and wire through from the other end. Voilà!

Bead chain in chandelier arm.

Reviving the Three-Arm, Mogul-Socket Floor Lamp

Gee, even the name is frightening! Here's a project that people with rewiring experience may hesitate to tackle. It shouldn't be all that daunting, though, and if you follow the steps and refer to the illustrations, it's downright simple.

Lamps of this type make up the majority of the floor lamps you'll run into. They usually have two switches: one that controls the mogul socket (the large socket that holds the big three-way bulb in the center) and a rotary switch lower down. In the first position, the lower switch turns on a bulb in one arm, in the second a bulb in two arms, and in the third a bulb in all three arms. If one or more bulbs fail to light, this switch is the culprit.

MATERIALS & TOOLS

- Screwdriver
- Pliers or small wrench
- Rotary switch

- Electrical cord
- Wire stripper
- Wire nuts

---

1. To open the cluster head, find that little screw that holds the top of the cluster to the bottom. Remove it with a screwdriver and tip the top to one side. You might have to exert some effort, but the top will pop loose.

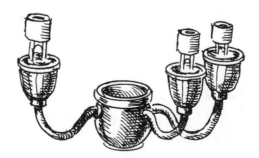

Cluster head.

2 Disconnect all the wires. What?! It looks like a den of snakes in there! How will you ever get everything back in place? Don't worry about it. Trust me. Just carefully separate all the wires by removing the wire nuts, or unwrapping the tape, and untwisting the ends.

Look at what you've got: two wires that run to each arm, two that run to the mogul socket, two that supply the power (the cord), and three that run to the rotary switch. Three? Yep, but don't panic. Pull the old cord out from the bottom.

3 To remove the old rotary switch, begin by removing the knurled nut on the outside. If you can't turn it, loosen the regular nut on the inside with a pair of pliers or a small wrench; then the knurled nut will come off easily. Pull the old switch out.

4 The replacement rotary switch will also have two nuts: one regular and one knurled. First, unscrew the knurled one and take it off; the other nut stays on. Push the switch through the hole and adjust the amount of the switch sticking through the head by positioning the nut on the inside. Replace the knurled nut and tighten it with your fingers. Then, while holding the switch with one hand, securely tighten the inside nut against the side of the head. This will lock the switch in place. Don't try tightening the outside nut with pliers. You'll leave gouges in it and scratch the head.

5 Feed the new cord (about 10 feet for a floor lamp) through to the cluster. Tie a knot in it to keep tension off the connections. Leave enough slack to work with and strip the ends, baring the wires.

REPLACING THE MOGUL SWITCH

If the switch in the mogul socket ever goes bad, the entire socket has to be replaced. With the top of the cluster off, first unscrew the knob on the outside of the shade holder that covers the socket. Take the nut off the nipple that holds the socket to the top (or unscrew the whole socket if it's threaded to the cluster top), and pull the socket out. It's replaced in the same manner and wired as previously described (see "Reviving a Table Lamp," pages 142–144).

6 Reconnect all the wires. This is a little awkward. The wires from that mogul socket have to go into this mix, and somehow they have to be held close to the rest of the wires while you work. If there's no one to hold them for you, tip the whole mess into your lap and work in that position.

Look at the illustration for guidance and connect the wires as follows:

a. Twist together the green switch wire, one mogul socket wire, and one wire from the cord. Put a wire nut on this combination.

b. Combine the red switch wire with one wire from each of any two arms. Attach with wire nut.

c. Connect the black switch wire to one of the wires from the third arm.

d. Now you've got five wires left: one from each arm, one from the mogul, and one from the cord. Connect all of these wires together with a wire nut.

That completes the wiring. Now all you have to do is snap the top back on and replace the screw.

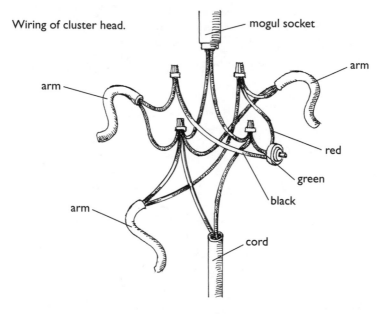

Wiring of cluster head.

mogul socket

arm

arm

arm

red

green

black

cord

Conversions

Back in chapter 4 I advised you to buy bridge lamps when you could, and I promised to show you how to adapt them to accept a more attractive shade. I also promised to show you how to convert a regular floor lamp to a bridge lamp.

At this point, you might wonder why you would want to do either. Good shades are costly. So what alternatives are there, other than re-covering a shade yourself? Exactly — converting a lamp to accept a more attractive (and cheaper) type of shade.

The Uno Adapter

Bridge lamps have sockets that are threaded on the outside to accept a screw-on paper or fabric shade. By purchasing an *Uno adapter* and screwing it on in place of the original shade, the lamp will be able to hold a vintage glass shade. These shades are plentiful and found in most any shop for a few dollars. Make sure that the *fitter* size (the diameter of the small end of the shade) is 2¼ inches — the size of a standard Uno adapter — and you're home free. If you can't find the adapters locally, see the source list at the back of the book.

Uno adapter.

Floor to Bridge

Talk about expensive! You practically need a second mortgage to buy a nice fabric shade for a standard cluster-head, mogul-socket floor lamp. This, combined with the loathing associated with having to rewire one of these monsters, scares most dealers away from purchasing them. That's fortunate for us, because we can usually snatch them up for a few bucks.

A number of companies (see the sources list) sell replacement bridge heads (also known as bridge arms). They have a ¼ IP thread, which, coincidentally, is the thread size of the pipe in a standard floor lamp. You see where we're going here? Just unscrew the entire cluster assembly, and screw the new bridge arm on in its place. Attach a new socket (with Uno threads), an adapter, and a glass shade, and you've got a bridge lamp.

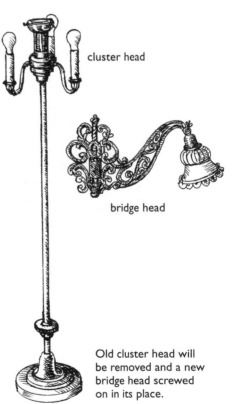

cluster head

bridge head

Old cluster head will be removed and a new bridge head screwed on in its place.

Oil Lamp Conversions

I don't advocate drilling holes or altering oil lamps in any way that permanently converts them to electric usage only. There's no point in doing that, since there are adapters to change almost any burner to electric:

▶ **Adapters with nipples** screw into the collar of the lamp where the burner was. The nipple has a ⅛ IP thread, onto which a standard socket can be screwed.

▶ **Wired burners** fit the majority of oil burners. Here again, just take the burner with the wick out, and screw the electric one in place.

The easiest and least destructive oil lamp conversions are made with readily available adapters.

A READY SIZE REFERENCE

Common thread sizes
(they don't make any sense at all, but you need to know them)

▶ ¼–27   Measures ¼ inch. It's the size of the thread that fits a finial.

▶ ⅛ IP   Measures ⅜ inch. It's the thread used in ordinary sockets to attach to the lamp pipe or nipple. It's also the pipe's size.

▶ ¼ IP   Measures ½ inch. It's what the pipes in floor lamps, bridge arms, and cluster heads use.

Oil lamp burner and adapter sizes

▶ 00   Measures ⅝ inch.

▶ No. 1   Measures ⅞ inch.

▶ No. 2   Measures 1¼ inches.

▶ No. 3   Measures 1¾ inches.

Vase Conversions

Without drilling a hole (and ruining it), any vase can be quickly converted into a lamp. This is an especially good use for a glass vase that has chips around the mouth and would otherwise be discarded. The vase caps are available in sizes ranging from about 1¼ to 8½ inches.

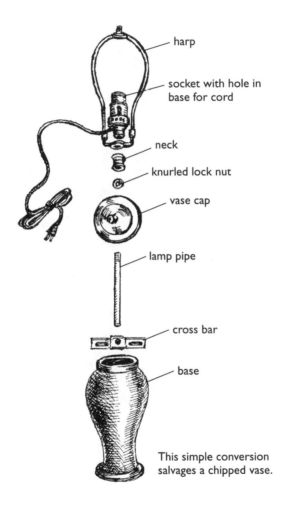

This simple conversion salvages a chipped vase.

resurrecting frames and mirrors

What could be better than frames and mirrors? They bring light and life to our walls, and it seems we never have quite enough of either. In this chapter, I'll give you some pointers on repairing these wondrous creations, so the next time you find a frame or mirror whose prime seems long past, you'll be able to restore it to its former glory in no time.

Fabulous Frames

Humans' earliest attempts at decorating might have been wall paintings in caves. From the time of these prehistoric cave drawings to the present, we have adorned our walls with some sort of ornamentation. Today there's a constant demand for prints, paintings, mirrors, or anything else that might embellish the uninteresting blank spaces in our lives. Fortunately, there are a number of tricks you can use to help satisfy this demand.

Maybe you picked it up after an auction or maybe it was thrown in with some better ones that you bought, but somehow you've acquired a totally dilapidated, completely destroyed frame. What a find! You probably got it for nothing, or close to it. Although it may appear worthless to others, we can turn it into something of usefulness and value. In this section I'll give you the how-to lowdown for four common operations: dividing up stacked frames, repairing frames ornamented with gesso (a mixture of glue and plaster), cutting down a damaged frame to a smaller size, and adapting a frame to make a shadow box.

Salvaging Stacked Frames

Damaged composite, sectional, or stacked frames are the fastest and easiest to repair. These frames are made up of two to four individual, graduated components nested one within the other. They're usually from the nineteenth century, and the outer section (made from wood covered with gesso) is often too far gone to salvage. The inner, more recessed pieces — being less exposed to wear — are often intact. By dismantling the frame, sometimes two or more usable sections are obtained.

MATERIALS & TOOLS

- Claw hammer or end cutters
- Wood filler or epoxy putty
- Paintbrush
- Black paint

---

1 Turn the frame over and find the nails that hold the sections together. There will be two to four fasteners driven through the edge of each section into the next section.

2 Remove the nails. If you can grasp the heads of the nails, pull them out. Since they're usually embedded in the wood, it's often simpler just to cut them with a pair of end cutters (a type of pliers).

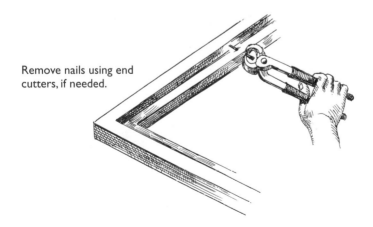

Remove nails using end cutters, if needed.

3 Once the nails are removed or cut, the sections come apart easily. You now have several individual frames of different sizes. (Don't discard the outer frame that's missing all the gesso, at least not yet. You might be able to use it later [see page 155].)

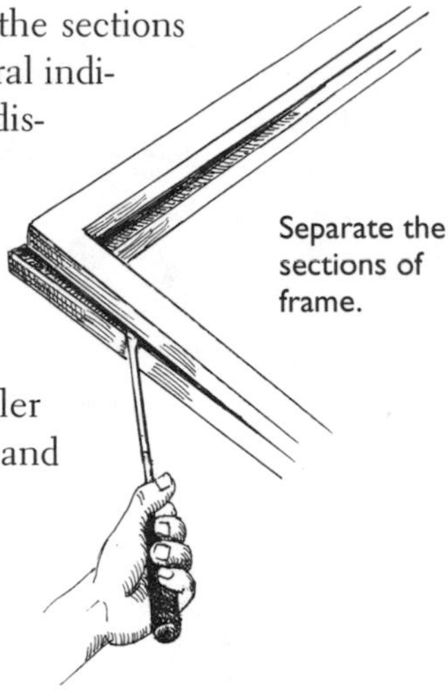

Separate the sections of frame.

4 Remove the remnants of the nails, fill the nail holes with a little wood filler or a dab of epoxy putty, wait for it to dry, and paint the edges black.

Repairing Gessoed Frames

The most common substance used for ornamentation on picture and mirror frames is a material called *gesso*, which is a mixture of glue and plaster. Over time, this substance cracks, chips, and falls off in big chunks. If it's a really nice frame and only a few areas of gesso are missing, you might want to try molding a patch for the missing material.

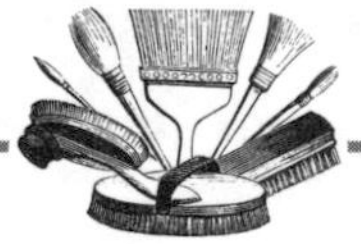

MATERIALS & TOOLS

- Cooking oil spray
- Epoxy putty
- Single-edge razor blade
- Soapy water

1 You'll notice that the design on an ornate frame is repeated over and over. Find an area on the frame where the design is intact and matches what would be in the missing section.

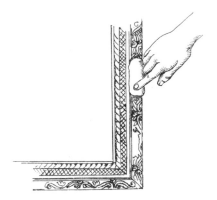

2 Make a mold. Spray the design you need to match with a nonstick cooking oil. Be sure to shield the spot where the repair will be made; otherwise, the repair material won't stick. Press a strip of epoxy putty over the design. Make the mold slightly longer than the space that you're going to fill, and about ¼ inch thick. In about 30 minutes, lift it off.

3 Fill the gap. The spot you're patching must be clean and the wood exposed. Fill the gap with a lump of epoxy putty, making sure it's level with the highest part of the surrounding design.

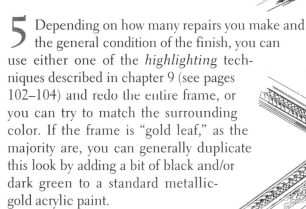

4 Spray your mold with some more oil, and press it facedown into the soft putty. Keep the mold in place for only a few minutes, then remove. With a razor blade, trim any excess putty that may have been squeezed out of the sides of the mold. Allow the epoxy to cure the required time, and then remove any remaining oil from the frame with soapy water.

5 Depending on how many repairs you make and the general condition of the finish, you can use either one of the *highlighting* techniques described in chapter 9 (see pages 102–104) and redo the entire frame, or you can try to match the surrounding color. If the frame is "gold leaf," as the majority are, you can generally duplicate this look by adding a bit of black and/or dark green to a standard metallic-gold acrylic paint.

Out of the Pantry, onto the Frame

If you have no epoxy putty and need to patch just a small area, a modified recipe for children's modeling clay will work. Here's the formula:

    1 part baking soda
    1 part cornstarch
    A little water
    Water-soluble wood glue

1. Mix the baking soda and cornstarch in a small saucepan. Add enough water to make a paste and cook over medium heat, stirring continuously until it begins to form a stiff dough. Remove the warm dough from the pan, add a few drops of glue, and work it in with your fingers.

2. Use modeling clay instead of epoxy putty to make the mold, spraying the design with oil as before. Because the clay mold will be pliable, it must be about 1 inch thick. Because it doesn't harden like the epoxy, the clay mold can be used several times.

3. Spread a little glue on the bare wood and allow it to dry until tacky. Fill the gap with a lump of dough, and press the greased mold onto the dough. Remove the mold and trim the patch. This substance dries slowly but dries hard, so be sure to make any needed adjustments before it dries completely.

Two-Cut Frame Restoration

Some time ago, I stood shaking my head sadly at a wonderful frame that someone had leaned against a cellar wall and left to rot. The side against the floor was ruined. The dampness had caused the gesso to soften and fall off. There was no chance of rebuilding that.

Then it struck me that it could still be a wonderful frame, half its original size, by making two simple cuts. Even if more than one side is damaged, you can almost always find enough good material in a bad frame to make a smaller one.

MATERIALS & TOOLS

- Block of wood
- Hammer
- Straightedge or other tool for marking a 45-degree angle

- Small saw
- Tacks

1 The bad side (side **A**) is removed by tapping it apart at the corners with a block of wood and a hammer. The corners are usually held together by just a few tacks. Discard side **A**. Then detach one remaining corner. Separate the frame at the points where sides **C** and **D** meet.

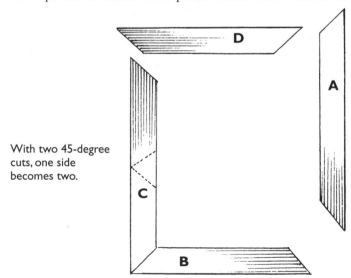

With two 45-degree cuts, one side becomes two.

2 Cut side **C** exactly in the middle, being sure to make the cut at a 45-degree angle. Leave **C** attached to **B**. Reattach the first corner by moving side **D** down, and tack it to the new angle on remaining side **C**.

3 Flip the section that you removed from the original side **C** around and cut a 45-degree angle. This piece now becomes the new side **A**. Complete the reconstruction by tacking new side **A** to **B** and **D**.

The new frame is exactly one-half the size of the original.

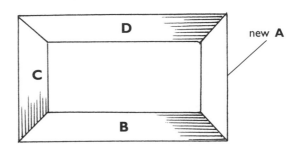

RESCUING AN OIL PAINTING

Have you ever seen oil paintings with big jagged holes in them sold at auction? They didn't bring much, did they? By employing the same technique used in the two-cut frame restoration, an oil on canvas can be saved. Often, an area of the painting that can stand on its own is undamaged.

Pry the tacks out of the stretcher to which the canvas is attached, removing as many tacks as necessary to cut the stretcher down to a size to accommodate the "new" smaller painting. Usually you can leave the canvas attached to the stretcher on one side. Now disassmble, cut, and renail the stretcher back together at the corners as was done in the two-cut frame restoration. Cut away the damaged part of the painting and retack to the rebuilt framework.

How to Make a Victorian Shadow Box

You can build a lovely shadow box using the simplest of tools. They're great for displaying items that have too much depth for conventional framing techniques. My favorite subjects for this treatment are fancy ladies' fans, but almost anything becomes special when framed this way.

MATERIALS & TOOLS

- A frame with glass
- Strip of lath (thin board that measures about 1⅜ inches wide by ³⁄₁₆ inch thick)
- Saw
- Wood glue
- Clamps

- Paintbrush
- Flat black paint
- Foam board
- Straight pins
- Hot-glue gun (optional)
- White glue for paper

---

1 With the frame facedown on the work surface, hold a piece of lath to the frame and mark it so that when cut, it will fit inside the frame, against the glass. Follow the same procedure for all four sides. We'll call these the **A** strips. Cut them so that the end of one strip butts against the side of the next.

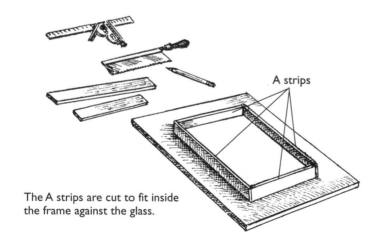

A strips

The A strips are cut to fit inside the frame against the glass.

2 With the **A** strips temporarily in place, mark and cut lath to fit against the outside of the **A** strips — these will rest against the frame. As before, the ends of these strips should butt against each other. We'll call these the **B** strips.

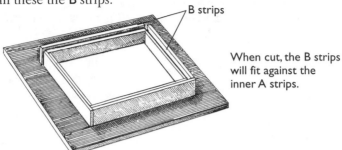

B strips

When cut, the B strips will fit against the inner A strips.

3 Put a bead of glue between each pair of **A** and **B** strips and clamp them together. After clamping, remove them from the frame until the glue dries.

4 Paint the strips flat black and let them dry.

5 With the clean glass in place, put a line of glue on the frame or the bottom edges of the **B** strips and put the paired **AB** strips in place. Put some weight, like a heavy book, on top of the strips until dry.

Glue and clamp sections.

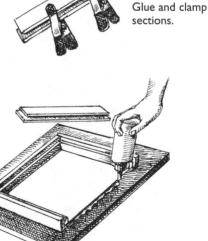

Glue the strips to the frame.

6 Cut a piece of foamboard to fit inside the **B** strips (it will be the length and width of the glass minus the combined width of the **A** strips), so that it rests on top of the edges of the **A** strips. Paint the foam board flat black.

7 For a really elegant look, the foam board and the strips can be coated with glue and covered with fabric. Velvet, though expensive, makes a striking display.

8 Mount the display item on the foam board. A fan can be mounted with straight pins pushed through the foam board and bent over on the back. Heavier objects can be wired in place or glued to the backing. A hot-glue guns works best for this, but put the glue on the object first so as not to melt the foam.

9 To stiffen the back and to hold everything in place, cover any pins or wire that come through the foam board with a second, larger sheet of foam board. Glue the second sheet of foam board over the first, and to the edges of the **B** strips, using a "tacky" glue that's made to adhere to paper and wood. Weight it until dry.

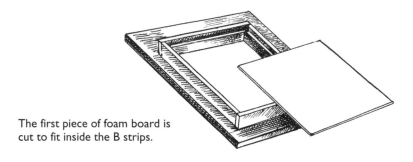

The first piece of foam board is cut to fit inside the B strips.

SUGGESTIONS FOR SHADOW BOXES

The list of objects suitable for display in a shadow box is practically endless. You're only limited by your creativity. Here are some of my recent favorites:

- ▸ Vintage can openers
- ▸ Bottle caps
- ▸ Fans
- ▸ Flow Blue saucer
- ▸ Straight razor with a shaving brush

I even framed a small art pottery vase that was so damaged that it was irreparable. Displayed in a shadow box, it brought a hefty sum.

Marvelous Mirrors

Do you know anyone whose home has no mirrors? Mirrors aren't there so much to reflect our images as they are to reflect our tastes. Mirrors add decorative touches and enlarge the spaces they occupy. Like framed pictures, mirrors are consistently good sellers in antiques shops.

I always keep a mirror or two in my shop. When I sell one, I make up another. Of course when I can buy a nice mirror, I do, but nine times out of ten they bring bigger prices than I'm willing to pay at auctions — unless, of course, the silver reflective surface is in bad shape. We'll talk about that shortly. First, let's discuss simple mirror mounting.

The Floating Mirror

Mirrors really do float in their frames. *Floating* refers to a method of mounting that allows the mirror some room within the frame; that is, the mirror is slightly smaller than the mounting space. There's a good reason for this, too. If the mirror were tight in the frame, the normal contraction and expansion of the wood (caused by variations in temperature and humidity) would squeeze the mirror. This could result in the corners of the frame being forced apart, or, if the frame is really sturdy, could crack the mirror itself.

The thicker the mirror and the more massive the frame, the more likely this is to occur. Thin mirrors (about ⅛ inch) will flex more and are unlikely to cause such a problem. If you get a thick mirror (¼ inch) custom-cut to fit into a frame (surprisingly inexpensive, and almost any glass company will do it, usually while you wait), have it sized ¼ inch smaller than the frame. This allows for ⅛ inch of play, all around.

WHO IS THE FAIREST OF THEM ALL?

Whenever I acquire or rebuild an ornate, heavy frame, I consider it a candidate for a mirror. You really can't justify putting a mediocre picture in an elaborate frame. And because finding a good oil painting at a reasonable price is unlikely, a mirror is the perfect solution.

If you have an exceptional frame and you don't want to bother with a mirror, though, you're better off trying to sell the empty frame than you are filling it with cheap or inappropriate artwork.

Mounting a Mirror

The old-fashioned method of keeping a mirror in the frame, while allowing it some movement and not scratching it, involves the use of small, wedge-shaped pieces of wood. They're easy to make.

As always, I hate asking you to buy specialized tools, but in this case you'll do yourself a big favor by purchasing something called a *brad setter*, or *framer's pliers*. This instrument has an adjustable head that fits most frames. It allows the brad (or nail) to be safely pushed into the frame, not pounded in. Believe me, hammers (even little bitty, I'll-be-real-careful-and-barely-tap-it hammers) should not be used around mirrors. A brad setter will pay for itself several times over by preventing disasters. (See the source list at the back of the book if you can't find one locally.)

MATERIALS & TOOLS

- Several small blocks of wood (¾ x ¾ x 1 inch)
- Dull knife
- Hammer

- Brads
- Wood glue
- Brad setter, or framer's pliers

---

1 Take a small block of wood, about ¾ × ¾ × 1 inch, and stand it on end. Place a not-so-sharp instrument, such as an old dull knife, against the end, corner to corner, and whack it with a hammer. You now have two wedges. Make enough wedges to install them every 8 inches or so around the frame.

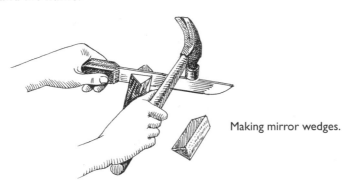

Making mirror wedges.

2 Check the fit of your wedges before you install them permanently. Remember, the glass should be able to move slightly within the frame, so you don't want the wedges crammed in there too tightly. When positioned properly, the mirror will be able to move a little side-to-side, but not too much back-and-forth. You might have to trim the wedges a bit on one or both sides to get just the right fit.

3 Start the brad by tapping it into the wedge before you place the wedge. (It's a good idea to coat one side of the wedge with glue also.) Now position the wedge, adjust the jaws of the framer's pliers, and squeeze the handle, forcing the brad into the frame. Work your way around the frame like this, placing a wedge every 8 inches or so.

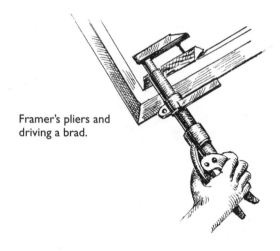

Framer's pliers and
driving a brad.

THIN MIRRORS

Wedges aren't necessary for mirrors that are thinner than 1/4 inch — you can mount these as you would a piece of ordinary glass, using push points (available where window glass is sold) or brads to hold the mirror tightly against the frame. Be sure to place a layer of cardboard between the nails and the back of the mirror to avoid scratching the coating with the pliers, though.

Hanging Hardware

Usually, screw eyes are sufficient to hold the average hanging mirror. Make sure the wire and the eyes are appropriate to the weight of the mounted mirror.

Place the eyes about one-fourth of the way down on each side of the frame, tap them gently to start, then screw them into the wood with pliers.

A common mistake made by those unfamiliar with the process is failure to securely and properly wrap the ends of the picture wire. See the accompanying illustration for the correct method.

The end of the picture wire is passed through the eye twice before it's wrapped around itself.

HANGING EXCEPTIONALLY HEAVY MIRRORS

More than one heavy mirror has come crashing to the floor because a screw eye pulled out of the frame. Even with large eyes having relatively long screws, the weight of the mirror might be too great for just two fasteners. If the frame seems a little thin or weak for the size of the mirror, or if you're concerned about the ability of two eyes to provide good support, use the method illustrated here. This will distribute the weight to four points on the frame.

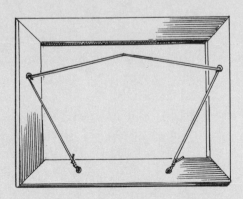

The wire is wrapped around the upper eyes once, then drawn through the lower eyes twice before being wrapped around itself. (See previous illustration.)

Beveled Mirrors

Beveled mirrors are a lot prettier than flat ones, but because they're custom-made to fit a frame, they're expensive. Here are three money-saving tricks you can use to lessen this expense:

1. **Buy standard-sized beveled mirrors.** Most glass shops keep on hand some premade beveled-edge mirrors that are cheaper than custom-made. If you've got a nice frame that's too large for a premade mirror, consider resizing the frame, using the methods described on pages 157–158).

2. **Strip the mirror and have it resilvered.** If you've bought a beveled mirror that's in poor condition, you can get it resilvered. Check the Yellow Pages of your phone book under "Mirrors" or "Glass" — you'll come up with at least one professional who does this work. It isn't an inexpensive job, but you can usually get a discounted price if you're willing to do some of the dirty work yourself. (See the "Stripping Mirrors" box.)

3. **Try the "mirror, mirror" trick.** The final alternative, and the one that's used more often than you might think, is the use of doubled mirrors. Simply strip and thoroughly clean the back of the beveled mirror. Have a thin, flat mirror cut to the same size (this is much cheaper than resilvering!), and mount it behind and flat against the stripped mirror.

STRIPPING MIRRORS

A strong paint remover will dissolve the tarry substance that covers the silver on the back of a mirror. Flow it on, let it sit, and scrape it off with a plastic scraper. Don't try to use razor blades or metal scrapers for this task — any scratches will be visible when silvered.

Although the coating of silver is extremely thin, it's tough to remove. Paint remover has little effect. Do you recall what we used for cleaning old silver plate in chapter 11? That's right, muriatic acid — it will remove the old silver coating. Apply it with very fine (0000) steel wool or a soft bristle brush, then rinse thoroughly. Clean with alcohol to remove any lingering traces. The mirror is now ready to deliver to the silverer's shop.

▸16◂

furniture repair for people with few tools

I'm no George Grotz, and this chapter won't turn you into one, either. If you don't know who *he* is, perhaps you shouldn't be messing around with furniture at all. Actually, Mr. Grotz, and a number of others, have written some great books on furniture repair and restoration. A trip to your local library or bookstore will allow you to share their abundant knowledge. (See the suggested reading list for some of my favorites.)

This chapter is for those of you who don't have unlimited budgets for tools, don't have big workshops, and can't spend all day fooling around with a wobbly leg. A lot of common problems have quick-and-easy fixes. Get your beginner's toolbox ready, and let's tackle them!

BEGINNER'S TOOL BOX

You'll need these general-purpose tools if you're going to attempt even the most elementary furniture repairs.

- Claw hammer
- Package of single-edge razor blades
- Flexible rule (tape measure)
- An inexpensive ¼ inch electric drill
- At least four drill bits: ⅛ inch, 3/16 inch, ¼ inch, and ½ inch (with ¼-inch shaft)
- Medium-sized standard and Phillips head screwdrivers
- Assorted grades of sandpaper
- Wood glue
- About 5 feet of nylon rope
- Assorted wood-color "putty" sticks
- Nail set
- Tack puller

Loose Stretchers

If a chair's legs sprawl out when you sit in it, the chair probably has loose *stretchers* — the pieces of wood that connect all the legs and brace the chair. If you want a quick fix for a stretcher that isn't too loose, skip steps 1 and 2.

1 Remove the stretcher. If it's really loose, you can spread the legs apart and pull the stretcher out. If one side is still stuck, place a padded block of wood against the leg and strike it lightly with a hammer; this will break the bond of the old glue. Clean the glued ends (and the holes in the legs) with coarse sandpaper, and apply some new wood glue.

Hold the stretcher, and tap the leg.

2 Reinsert the ends of the stretcher into the legs and apply a tourniquet. (The tourniquet is in lieu of a web clamp, a handy tool but a little pricey.) Here's how: Loop a length of nylon rope around the legs and tie a knot. Insert a stick in the knot and twist, drawing the legs together. To stop the rope "clamp" from untwisting, allow the end of the stick to wedge itself under the bottom of the chair. Leave the tourniquet in place until the glue dries.

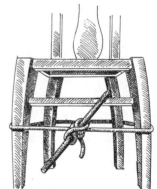

Apply a tourniquet.

3 So that the repair will remain intact, drive a small finishing nail into the leg and through the end of the stretcher. Be careful! Don't use a large-diameter nail that might split the leg, and don't use one long enough to go all the way through. Drive the nail in from the back of the leg, where it's less visible. Sink the head with a nail set and fill the small hole with matching wood putty.

Sagging, Loose, Ill-Fitting Drawers

In a lot of older pieces, such as chests of drawers and dressers, the drawers don't fit very well anymore. When you shove them in, they don't stop where they should, they tip down in the back (making them hard to open when full), and they don't slide easily. These problems are easily fixed.

1 Examine the drawer guides for wear. You can call them guides, slides, or glides, but in any case, these are the strips of wood on each side of the chest that the sides of the drawers rest on. If they're badly worn, it's a simple procedure to turn them over.

2 If you can get the claw of your hammer or some other sturdy prying tool in there and force it between the strip of wood and the side of the chest, you'll be able to pop the guide off. Normally, guides are held in place with a couple of nails and some old, crumbling glue.

Remove drawer guide.

3 Knock the nails flush with the guides, and turn the guides over so that what was the bottom is now the top — the top will contact the drawer. Run a bead of glue along the guides, and nail them back in place. You might need someone to hold a book or something else that won't scratch against the side as you pound. Rub a candle, some paraffin, or a bar of soap on the drawer where it makes contact. The drawers should now slide easily, be tighter, and won't sag toward the back.

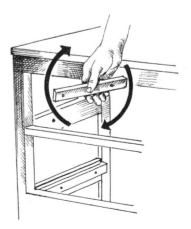

4 Check the stops. On a lot of furniture, there are little wooden blocks that stop the drawer from going in too far or keep the drawer from being pulled all the way out. Often these are missing, so the drawer doesn't fit flush with the front of the chest. Look closely on the inside of the piece. It's unlikely that all the stops will be missing. They might be in back, or up front along that strip of wood that separates the drawer compartments.

5 Replace missing stops. Measure one of the stops, and make new ones approximately the same size. If you can't cut the little blocks yourself, small strips of wood in various dimensions are available at most home supply stores. Even better, go pick up a few handfuls of scraps at the local lumberyard or cabinetmaker's shop.

6 Normally you can see where the old stops were, or you can estimate appropriate placement from those that are still there. A drop of glue and a short nail are all you need to secure them. Drive a nail all the way through each block before you try to nail them in place inside the chest.

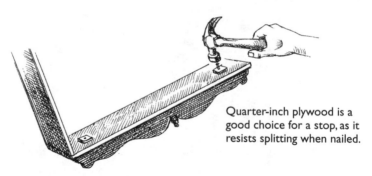

Quarter-inch plywood is a good choice for a stop, as it resists splitting when nailed.

Bubbled or Missing Veneer

When small areas of veneer have raised, forming little humps, they usually can be reglued fairly easily. Replacing small areas of missing veneer is also quite simple. You can use a bit of veneer you've salvaged from some other piece of furniture, a piece from a less noticeable area of the same furniture, or, as I do, a piece from a sample or starter kit available from a woodworker's supplier. (See the source list at the back of the book for suggestions.)

Bubbled Veneer

1 Using a single-edge razor blade and following the grain, make a cut through the veneer, spanning the entire length of the blister.

2 With the tip of a knife or other flat instrument, force some glue into each side of the cut. Press the veneer down with the heel of your hand, squeezing out the excess glue. Remove the excess with a damp rag, place a piece of waxed paper over the repair, and weight or clamp it. Let it dry overnight. If the paper sticks to the slit, it usually can be removed by pulling the wax paper back and sliding the edge of a razor blade, at an angle, gently against the surface.

Missing Veneer

1 Lay the veneer "patch" on top of the area to be repaired, matching the grain pattern as closely as possible. Cut through the new and old veneer, slightly beyond the edges of the missing material. (This will ensure that your patch is exactly the same size as the area to be patched.) Remove the old veneer.

2 Replace the missing material. Spread a small amount of glue on the underside of the veneer patch, position the piece, and press it down, squeezing out the excess glue. Remove the excess with a damp rag, place a piece of waxed paper over the repair, and weight or clamp it. Let it dry overnight.

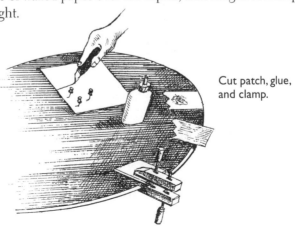

Cut patch, glue, and clamp.

Making an Invisible Patch

Gouges, missing wood, and nail and screw holes from previous botched repair jobs can be repaired and the patch neatly hidden. You see, the eye and the brain have to work together, but like co-workers everywhere, they don't always cooperate. Sometimes, the eye can fool the brain. The technique of trompe-l'oeil ("deceive the eye") has been used by artists for centuries. We can join this long tradition when filling a hole in an obvious place on a piece of furniture.

1 Fill the hole. It's not all that important what you fill it with. There are lots of wood fillers available. Use something that can be stained, as it's unlikely you'll get a perfect color match otherwise. No matter what material you use, in fact, it's unlikely you'll get a perfect match.

2 This is where I draw the line, literally. Since you're not going to get a perfect color match, you need to do something to minimize the contrast. If the wood's grain continues right through the patched area, your eyes won't be drawn immediately to that spot and your mind might be none the wiser. Draw the lines with a soft lead or colored pencil.

Draw grain on filler patch.

Loose Legs and Floppy Tops

I'm referring to the unfortunate condition of various parts of furniture that have, over time, become semidetached. Two fastening methods lend themselves to quick-and-easy correction.

Loose Dowel Pins

Furniture that was pinned together, using wooden dowels and glue, can become wobbly when the glue breaks down and the pins become worn or broken. If they break off in one or both holes, just drill them out to a larger size and insert new dowel pins. If you do a lot of furniture work, it will be worth your while to buy a selection of these pins in different sizes.

For the occasional repair, a section of wooden handle from one of the disposable foam paintbrushes I rave about will suffice. You can cut a few glue-grooves, or *flutes*, in it by raking it across the teeth of a saw before you cut it to length.

PREPARING FOR REUPHOLSTERY

Way back in chapter 4, I advised you to buy upholstered furniture that needs re-covering. If you and an upholsterer can reach an agreement, you can save considerable money by doing the unskilled work yourself.

1. With a sharp razor blade, cut the fabric away from the frame. Don't remove the material that covers the padding and the springs unless the upholsterer has agreed to this. The upholsterer might prefer to do this task unassisted.
2. Remove the tacks or staples. No matter how much of the stuffing the upholsterer wants to remove, you can bet you'll get a gold star for removing all the tacks or staples. It's a slow, nasty job, but with pliers and a tack puller, you can do it. (*Note:* This is the time to clean or refinish any exposed wood. You can't do it after the re-covering.)

Loose Screws

Sometimes people go to a lot of trouble trying to remedy this problem. They fill the old screw hole with wood or wood filler, or wrap something around the threads of the screw to make it tighter. Neither solution is very effective. Most of the time, simply using a larger diameter screw does the trick. Drywall screws in various lengths are great for this job. (Lubricating the threads of a screw with a little wax or soap makes it much easier to drive.)

REPAIRING WOVEN CHAIR SEATS

I've known dealers who have completely replaced — unnecessarily — splint seats because a few pieces of splint were broken or missing. I've been able to save the cost of this repair by just replacing the missing pieces.

Soak a section of splint A, which is a couple of inches longer than the missing section, to make it flexible, and then push A under the edge of piece B until the far end is even with the edge of piece C. Then, pushing the far end of A under C, work it forward under B until both ends are concealed.

selling

You've bought it and improved it or fixed it. Now it's time to sell it. If you're currently a dealer, you'll want to read these next chapters to help improve your business. If you're just getting into the business, or even thinking about it, this section will guide you through some of the decisions you'll need to make about where and how you sell, as well as what to do after the sale.

But what about those of you who are collectors or happy-go-lucky bargain hunters? Well, believe it or not, that's the way I started. In fact, I'd be willing to bet that more than half the dealers out there had no thought of going into business when they first started buying antiques. In some cases, collectors find that their collections become too large, or they might want to constantly upgrade the quality of their collection. For them, selling some of their acquisitions eventually becomes a necessity. Others, like me, discover that it's the hunt that intrigues them the most. To be able to dedicate time and money to searching and buying, we must sell.

If it sounds like the business end of all this is boring, think again. If you do it right, it can be profitable and fun. These next chapters will show you how to minimize your efforts and expenses while maximizing sales.

Do you know what you need to do to go into business? What are the advantages and disadvantages of setting up a shop in your home? What about those antiques malls? How do you encourage even frequent shoppers to keep coming back to look in your shop? How do you arrive at a fair price for your merchandise? Do you have to keep books and an inventory? These, along with many more frequently asked questions will be explored in this section. Put on your selling hat, and let's do some business!

▶17◀

where to sell

After you've accumulated enough merchandise and you're ready to go into business, one of the first things you'll need to do is decide where you're going to locate. Ultimately, only you can determine what's best for your particular circumstances, but looking at the pros and cons of the various choices might help you make that decision.

Seven Possible Locations for Selling

Years ago if you wanted to sell antiques, you converted the chicken coop or allocated the parlor to shop space. Today there are many other alternatives:

▶ A single-owner, rented shop
▶ A group shop or antiques mall
▶ The show circuit
▶ Renting space at a flea market
▶ A shop at your home
▶ Consignment selling
▶ Several minishops with public exposure but no rent

Without a doubt, these options don't cover all the possible nuances of doing business in every possible situation. You might choose to start in one mode and "graduate" to another. You might even decide to engage in business at several locations at the same time.

One of the best things about the antiques business is its flexibility. That and the ability to work into it slowly, with little investment, make it one of the most popular of sole ownerships. Can you think of any other business that has so many proprietors? Trust me — there's plenty of room for more!

A Single-Owner, Rented Shop

At one time or another, almost all of us have dreamed of being our own boss, of doing what we please when we please. An antiques shop might seem to fit that dream nicely, but be sure to look closely before you make the move.

PROS & CONS

+ You are your own boss. No one can tell you when to come or go, when to open or close.
+ No one tells you what types of merchandise you can stock or how you have to display it.
+ You can work on antiques between customers.
+ Pickers will start bringing things to you.
+ You can keep an eye on your merchandise.
– Overhead is a large expense. Will you be responsible for heat, lighting, water, and certain maintenance costs (like clearing the parking lot of snow) in addition to the rent? Will you have a lease?
– You're tied to the store. You can open and close as you please, but erratic hours discourage would-be customers. You can't get out and look for merchandise unless you close or hire someone.
– You have to do your own advertising and provide a sign for the outside of the store.
– You could have trouble keeping an entire building full of merchandise.

A Group Shop or Antiques Mall

Increasingly, this is where more and more dealers are locating.

PROS & CONS

+ Unless you're in a co-op, where you're required to spend some time, you don't have to be in your shop. You can come and go whenever you like.
+ Your rent covers all your expenses — no utilities or maintenance costs to worry about.
+ The lease on your space is very short-term, usually thirty days, so you can pull out quickly if you need to.
+ The mall owners are responsible for advertising.
+ Traffic through your shop will usually be greater than in a stand-alone building.
+ They do a lot of your paperwork, providing you with periodic printouts of sales and, in some cases, even filing state sales taxes for you.

- A space in a mall is more impersonal. If you enjoy the interaction with customers, it's limited here.
- There probably will be restrictions on the types of merchandise you can stock and how you can display it. Can you hang things from the ceiling? Are there walls for pictures? Are there receptacles for plugging in lamps?
- Although traffic is greater, so is competition, with many other dealers all around you.
- Although most center owners try hard, they simply can't watch everyone. You might have to provide locked cases for valuable smalls.
- You might have to pay a commission on sales.

The Show Circuit

If you don't want a "permanent" location, maybe attending several antiques and collectibles shows a year will better suit you. They're held in auditoriums, shopping centers, and other public facilities.

PROS & CONS

+ A chance to travel and meet people with similar interests.
+ You can schedule your selling time as you wish, doing as few or as many shows as you like. You aren't forced to keep a shop stocked.
+ You can specialize in your favorite antique or collectible. You don't have to appeal to a broad spectrum of collectors.
+ No overhead, except for your vehicle.
- All that packing and unpacking and repacking! (Don't forget about the sources of packing materials mentioned on page 64.)
- The really good shows, as well as motel accommodations, are sometimes booked as much as a year in advance. Be sure you make arrangements early!
- Breakage. No matter how carefully you pack, it seems that something always gets broken.
- You need a vehicle large enough to transport your entire stock, instead of a few pieces at a time, as you would in a shop.
- You might have to collect and file sales taxes for several states.

Antique
Show
July 5 & 6
Over
200
Dealers!

Renting Space at a Flea Market

Basically, the same pros and cons that apply to doing shows apply also to setting up at flea markets. There are a few unique to this type of selling, though.

PROS & CONS

+ No restrictions on what you sell.
+ At many flea markets, you can just show up. You don't have to reserve space long in advance.
- Because there are no restrictions, conditions and facilities may be less than desirable.
- Unlike buyers at shows or shops, people at flea markets expect to pay rock-bottom prices. They're in more of a yard-sale mode of buying.
- Many flea markets are held outdoors, so weather is sometimes prohibitive.

A Shop at Your Home

For some dealers this might seem to be the perfect arrangement, and in many ways it is. Don't overlook the drawbacks, though.

PROS & CONS

+ Low overhead. After all, this is part of your home, so most of the expenses will be there whether you're using it as shop space or not.
+ You might be able to deduct from your taxes certain expenses related to the business use of your home.
+ While tending the shop, you are still home. This can be good if you have children or other things going on around your house that need your attention. That includes refinishing or in other ways improving the antiques you sell.
+ You can be open anytime, earlier or later than your competitors. Holidays, weekends, evenings — it's your choice.
+ You might have more storage space at home, and you only need to transport things once.
- Your home becomes your business. It becomes difficult to get away from work. You can have people dropping in at all hours. You surrender some of your privacy.
- With the IRS, there's always a payback. What you deduct or depreciate today can come back to haunt you if you ever sell your home.
- You could have to go through all sorts of zoning boards to operate a business in a residential area. In fact, you might not be able to run a business out of your home at all.

- You will probably need more insurance. Don't overlook the liability aspects of having strangers roaming around your property, either. You should also have some concern for security, especially if you're away from home for any length of time.
- You might need another telephone line. Business rates are not the same as residential phone rates.

Consignment Selling

Of all the ways of being in the antiques business, selling your merchandise through a consignment shop is probably the simplest.

PROS & CONS

+ No commitment — you take it to the shop if and when you feel like it.
+ You can spread your merchandise around to several shops without incurring any additional expense as you would if you were renting space.
+ You can ease into the business to see how you like it. Do one piece. Do a dozen. See what sells best. Take your time and develop your skills and knowledge without the pressure of keeping a space fully stocked.
- Someone else controls what you can display.
- The commission rate can be so high that you have to set your prices accordingly. This makes you less competitive in an area where shops and dealers abound. Since you have no overhead, you might be able to live with a smaller profit margin, though. In some shops, however, you don't even set the final selling price.
- Space is limited. You won't always be able to place everything you acquire if you become very active in the business.
- You have to transport the merchandise twice, usually.

Several Minishops with Public Exposure but No Rent

In chapter 5, I mentioned that you could get into business without paying any rent or commissions. It takes a little legwork, but you *can* do this. Here's how it works:

Approach the owners of various establishments where a nice antique would add to the decor. It might surprise you to learn that your dentist, doctor, or veterinarian might welcome a vintage picture, a chair, or a lamp. Bed-and-breakfasts might jump at the chance to fill a vacant spot. Wallpaper-and-paint stores are especially responsive to accepting this type of display. You might place a restored trunk or a marbleized table there. Restaurants are another good option, especially small ones.

Once you've made a few contacts, you'll need to work out an arrangement for being paid. Most businesses are going to be reluctant to transact your business, collecting payment and taxes. Ask them to have the check made out to you or to contact you when a sale is imminent. Calculate the taxes for them, and include it in the price. In other words, make it as easy for them as possible and agree to replace the item when it's sold.

PROS & CONS

+ No overhead.
+ Lots of exposure.
+ You can do as much or as little as you like.
+ Places your merchandise in unexpected and noncompetitive environments.
− Limits the numbers and types of antiques you can place.
− Some shop owners may resist the idea. (Overcome this by showing them a piece and explaining how it will benefit their establishment.)
− You'll need to keep a "backup" for each article you place. (A shop owner might not appreciate having an empty display window once it's been filled.)

Your "loan" of antiques provides you with free display space and can be eye-catching window decoration.

▶18◀

how to get and keep customers

As I said in the introduction, there's a lot more to selling than just dumping your merchandise in a shop. If it were that simple, retail businesses would all look alike. Merchandise would simply be lined up on nondistinctive shelves in drab buildings.

Grocery stores and large retailers learned long ago that attracting prospective customers was only part of the formula for success. They found that the longer they could keep someone in the store, the more that person was likely to buy. And any successful retailer will tell you that repeat business is vital. In this chapter we'll study the principles of selling and learn how they can be applied in your enterprise.

Attracting Customers

You can't totally separate attracting customers from keeping them in the shop, because many of the things you do to entice them will also keep them there awhile. But you have to grab their attention first!

Advertising

If you're starting off small, it's unlikely that there's much room in your budget for advertising. If yours is an individual shop, though, some advertising is essential. You can't depend on walk-in traffic or word of mouth, especially in the beginning.

The trick is to make the most of your advertising budget. I haven't found ads placed in the classified section of newspapers to be an especially effective way of spreading the word. You're better off spending the little money you can to add your shop's name to one of the free flyers or advertising circulars that are left at various locations for public consumption.

If you can't find someone who produces these little take-along cards or leaflets, consider talking to other dealers in the area about what can be a very productive, cooperative approach to publicity: Create your own leaflets! The more shops that participate, the less each owner will have to contribute financially. Check the Yellow Pages under "Advertising." You'll be surprised at the number of firms that specialize in this type of thing. They can design, print, and in many cases even distribute for you. Of course, you can save more money by circulating them yourself.

If you do place ads, place them only in antiques-related publications. Because readers of these publications obviously share your interest in antiques you'll have an interested, captive audience. Visit some antiques centers, and you'll find a number of publications that fit this description. You'll find a few regional and nationally distributed periodicals in the suggested reading at the back of this book, but you might have more luck with a locally published version.

If your shop is in a group establishment, you won't have a lot of control over the kind of advertising done. So before you sign a rental agreement, ask the management of the center what type and how much advertising they do. Some advertise extensively, even using local television stations, while others do practically nothing. Get this information up front, and remember that large centers are in the business of renting space — selling your antiques will not necessarily be their top priority.

The Sign

If you're located in a stand-alone building or a shop situated among other stores, you need a big, eye-catching sign that says "Antiques." It doesn't have to say "Smith's Antiques" or something cute like "Ye Olde 1847 Stone Grist Mill Antiques Shoppe." For one thing, it costs money to put all those words on a sign, and people driving by don't give a hoot what you call your business as long as you sell antiques! You can put all that other information on a smaller sign on the door or in the window. Also, if you invest a lot of money in a sign and later sell the business, who'll buy the sign?

Stopping Traffic

You've picked a location that gets some traffic, you've advertised, and you have that big old "Antiques" sign where no one can miss it, but people keep driving by. Why is that? Maybe they don't know you're open. Since so many small shops conduct business only on certain days, people traveling by usually won't even slow down unless it's obvious that your shop is open. Here are a few helpful ways to assure them that you are open and to make them apply their brakes:

- Get one of those big flags that says "Open."
- Make sure your front windows are brightly lit. Hang some antique lighting fixtures or display some lamps that are turned on. You can't have too much light.
- Pack your windows full of merchandise.
- Drag some of your inventory outside. Nothing convinces people that you're open more than merchandise sitting out front.
- FREE! See how that word catches your eye. People love getting something for nothing. In the fall, make a deal with a farmer. Buy a wagonload of pumpkins. Give them away! Maybe a sign that reads "Free Apples and Cider" will pull them in. How about, "Free Coffee and Hot Chocolate"? None of these is terribly expensive, and they're guaranteed to stop traffic and encourage folks to linger.

EVEN IN A MALL, YOU NEED A SIGN

You might think that if you're located in a booth in a large center, you won't need a sign. That's not true. Your shop is a singular business, not just a tiny part of a larger whole. A sign will make your space stand out from all those others, and it doesn't have to be huge or expensive, either, since people are in the building looking for antiques.

Unlike the outdoor sign, the indoor sign should emphasize the individuality of your shop so people will remember it. Use a simple, easy-to-recall, but unusual name for your shop, and display it prominently.

Stopping Browsers

What if you don't have a shop, but only a nondescript space in a large antiques center? How do you convince browsers that they should stop at your booth? You can use a few tricks here, too:

▸ Light your booth as much as possible. You might not have many outlets, but use all you're allowed. Hang lights from the ceiling if you can. (Many dealers won't bother.)

▸ Regularly rearrange your booth, even if you haven't sold much. A lot of people stroll through these malls on a regular basis and pass by the spaces that appear not to have changed since the last time they looked.

▸ Dust every week. If it looks like things have been sitting around forever, people suspect there's a reason why.

▸ FREE! It works here, too, doesn't it?

▸ Individualize your space. Get that sign! Throw a rug on the floor, even if there's already carpeting.

▸ Put something interesting toward the back of the booth and call attention to it. Consider putting it in a box with a strategically placed sign that attracts the eye but isn't quite legible until the shopper *enters* the booth.

Keeping Them in the Shop and Encouraging Sales

Once you've attracted potential customers into your shop, you have to keep them there as long as possible. The longer they dally, the more likely they are to spot something they just can't live without. You could physically block their escape route, but a more subtle approach, appealing to all their senses, can be almost as effective. While sight and touch are fairly obvious points of attraction, don't neglect smell, sound, and taste.

Smell

The sense of smell is the most evocative of our senses. It triggers long-forgotten memories and creates images in our minds, so it's no wonder it can affect our moods. Use aroma in your shop to relax your customers and make them comfortable. You can do this in several ways:

▸ **Air fresheners.** Even if your shop is located in an open space in a large mall, a couple of those stick-on air fresheners placed inconspicuously can give your space a distinctive je ne sais quoi.

▸ **Potpourri.** This product comes in countless varieties and scents, and you can always find one that suits the season or the mood you're trying to create. But don't buy cheap stuff that makes your eyes water. I've been in shops where the scent was so overpowering that my clothes reeked of it an hour after leaving.

▸ **Sachet.** In the drawers of some of the furniture you display, place envelopes of pleasantly scented sachet. Sachet placed inside a restored trunk will help disguise the musty smell that seems to cling to them.

▸ **Natural smells.** If space permits, consider things like apples, fresh coffee, or a real Christmas tree.

▸ **The smell of clean.** No one objects to a clean smell. Your shop shouldn't smell antiseptically clean, like a hospital, but pleasantly clean. Oil soap and lemon oil have a clean scent, and the homemade cleaner mentioned in chapter 6 (page 70) imparts a pleasing aroma. (Clean, polished surfaces also appeal to the sense of touch.)

Sound

Consider for a moment what it is that you're selling in an antiques shop. Aside from the objects, what you're really dealing in is nostalgia. People often buy things that remind them of their childhoods or that harken back to a simpler time. Music enhances that atmosphere.

▸ Generic background music is better than nothing. It doesn't distract, and it may calm and soothe, but it doesn't motivate.

▸ You're selling antiques, so what you need is antique music! Re-recordings of music from early phonograph records is perfect. Some big-band tunes interspersed with an occasional rock-and-roll ballad from the 1950s will appeal to almost every generation. I visited one antiques mall that employs a piano player on weekends.

▸ If you have your own shop, you can control the music and almost custom-fit it to the customers in the shop at the time.

▸ If you're in a booth, suggest that management furnish music. If they won't, ask if you can keep a radio tuned softly to an "oldies" or classical station.

Taste

We already discussed the benefits of hot coffee, cocoa, apples, and cider, but that sort of thing isn't practical for everyone. Even in the smallest of spaces in the largest of centers, though, you can still make your patrons' visits tasty.

▶ **Nuts.** A bowl of nuts in their shells and a couple of nut crackers (and a waste basket) can be pretty messy, but it will slow a few folks down. While they're cracking nuts, they'll be glancing around your shop.
▶ **Candy.** A bowl of wrapped candies, placed well back from the entrance of a booth, or scattered around a larger shop in unexpected places, is a friendly gesture. It might sound ridiculous, but you shouldn't provide flavors that clash with the atmosphere you're trying to create. Root beer, chocolate, toffee, lemon drops, mellow mints, and caramels are good choices, while hard candies that are sour or tangy aren't.
▶ **Homemade cookies.** Not an everyday thing, for sure, but how can you go wrong with cookies on special occasions?

Appearances: The Most Important Thing You Can Do

You can furnish treats for their noses, lull them with music, and bribe them with food, but the single most important factor is how your shop looks. The possibilities are limitless.

Avoid Clutter

If your shop looks like a yard sale, people will expect yard-sale prices. If things are jumbled together, with no attempt at organization, some customers won't bother to dig through in search of something to buy.

In the same vein, if you have too much in your space, people may become overwhelmed. Although it's difficult to strike a balance between sparsity and overcrowding, strive to do so. You don't want customers to see everything in one glance, but you don't want them to overlook anything, either.

Artful Display

I can't teach you how to decorate your shop tastefully — that could be a book in itself. For the most part, personal taste and what you stock will determine how you present it. Here are some pointers:

- **Make use of all your space, including the ceiling.** A length of light chain hung from hooks that are securely fastened to the ceiling can display a remarkable variety of items. If you don't want to hang a lot of chains, hang a two-by-four from two chains and put some hooks on that. Don't hang things so low that shoppers will bang their heads, but a few tassels strategically placed overhead will gently brush them and direct their gazes upward.
- **Look through a few antiques malls.** Why do some shops look so much more inviting? Do they place lamps and glassware on one big table, like at a flea market, or do they arrange them on furniture and shelves?
- **Get a corner.** When you have a choice of mall space and the booths aren't separated by walls, a corner is always best, as it will provide you with an area to hang pictures, sconces, and mirrors, among other things.
- **Get an old fireplace mantel.** Paint it or marbleize it, and attach it to a back wall. Arrange items on it and place a large picture or mirror above it.

Attention to Detail

I've been in shops where everything seems to be done right. They're not overcrowded, they're organized, merchandise is tastefully displayed, but something just doesn't seem right. It could be that they've overlooked some of the small details that can set a shop apart.

- **Put doilies under lamps or other items.** You don't have to buy old ones. Discount store or even paper doilies are better than bare surfaces.
- **Beware of adhesive tags.** Use adhesive price tags only on things that can be cleaned easily of the sticky residue, never on something that will be damaged by the removal. Sales are often lost because of this simple oversight.

- **Conceal the unsightly.** If you use a folding table, or some other modern table as part of your display, conceal it with a tablecloth. A lace tablecloth with a pastel sheet underneath will suffice. (Worn or slightly stained table coverings are inexpensive at auctions.)
- **Don't use plain white-string tags for pricing.** Custom-printed tags are expensive but best. If you use the commercial variety, at least put some little stickers on the tags or use a novel rubber stamp with a pastel ink. By all means, don't use fluorescent colors! If you know or you're willing to learn just a little calligraphy, you can really add a nice touch. Even the most mundane object seems to take on greater value when embellished with a "special" price tag.

A Cheap, Easy-to-Make Price Tag

With pinking shears, cut small rectangles out of pieces of common brown-paper bag. Fold each rectangle, punch a hole in the corner, and tie with a bit of raffia or ribbon.

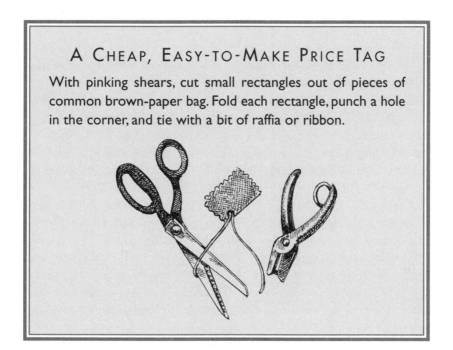

▸19◂

pricing your merchandise

Buying low and selling lower is not the conventional wisdom for becoming wealthy. Witness the breakneck speed of expansion of huge discount chains like Wal-Mart or Kmart, and you'll see what I'm getting at, though. With more and more antiques and collectibles dealers moving to large centers or malls, thus somewhat emulating the big discounters, the concept of "discount pricing" has spilled over into the antiques business. The mere act of clustering a lot of retailers in one spot sparks competition, which in turn tends to lower, or at least level, prices.

Beginners in the antiques trade find pricing to be one of the most challenging aspects of selling. Years ago, pricing was hard enough for the traditional "mom-and-pop" operation. Today, with hundreds of dealers in a single location, it's much worse. Price it too high, and it just sits. Price it too low, and it disappears before you know it. But at what kind of return?

It sure would be convenient if I could give you some formulas. Those big retailers use them. They can take all their expenses into consideration and multiply their wholesale costs by a certain percentage and know that they will make an adequate profit. That's an oversimplification, of course, but you get the general idea.

In this chapter, I hope I'll help you find a price that's right.

Pricing Practices to Avoid

The formulas that regular retailers use don't work in this business. For one thing, there are no standard wholesale prices. What you got for a buck at last week's estate sale costs you ten dollars at an auction this week.

I'd be remiss if I didn't offer you the benefit of what I have learned, though. First, we need to dispel some commonly held beliefs.

Double Your Money!

You'll hear dealers say that they like to double their money on any sale. There have even been books written suggesting it. But if you use that as a rule of thumb and apply it more or less across the board, you're headed for trouble.

For instance, using that one-dollar bargain as an example again: At retail, is it worth only two dollars? And the one you paid ten dollars for might never fetch twenty. Probably, somewhere between the two extremes is a fair value. When you sell, you can expect to make a huge profit (percentagewise) on the first example and just about break even on the second.

I'll Price It High — I Can Always Come Down

That's very true, and the key word here is *always*. Didn't your momma ever warn you about getting a "reputation"? If time after time you're asked for a better price and you consent to the reduction, word gets around that (1) your prices are too high, and (2) you always give in. With this strategy, you can't win.

I Don't Have to List Prices

How do you feel when that happens to you? Doesn't it feel like the proprietor is sizing you up? What if your offer is absurdly low? Are you afraid you'll embarrass yourself? What if you make an offer much higher than what the owner was expecting? If this practice doesn't annoy you, you're an exception. Don't do it.

BOOK VALUE REVISITED

We have already talked a little about price-and-identification guides (see page 37), but it's a subject worth revisiting. Dealers who price collectibles "by the book" usually get to keep those treasures for a long, long time. In fact, for some categories half the book price is more the norm. At the same time, pricing on a few rare items begins at the top value listed. So why bother looking at these books?

Well, perhaps most importantly, they help you recognize things. They also provide a range within which most buying and selling should normally take place. Finally, they're a good reference to quote when offering an item at a particular figure.

How *Do* You Set Prices?

Setting prices is serious business. It can mean the difference between success and failure. But while I can tell you exactly how to make a price tag, I can only offer you general advice on how to go about deciding what number to put on it.

Stop Feeling Guilty

The first thing novice dealers must do is stop feeling guilty about making a profit. Those who have never been involved in retail in any way sometimes have a hard time overcoming this. There's a gnawing feeling that paying one price and charging a higher one is somehow immoral.

It doesn't help to overhear people grumbling about how they "bet the owner paid less than half that!" as they walk through shops — they rarely buy anything. Never mind that to get some of your merchandise you stood all day in a cold drizzle while your toes slowly became numb. And never mind that you *enjoyed* it. The point is, if they wanted to they could have been standing out there with you.

Price Yours Lower

You can sell anything at the right time and place, but to sell consistently in a competitive market, your merchandise has to be better, cheaper, or unique. If your stock reflects your ability to find the better and the unique, then you can pretty much charge whatever the traffic will bear. If, however, your inventory is fairly representative of what's generally available on the market (to you and your customers), you'd better have the lowest price around.

Fortunately for you, if you follow the suggestions in this book you'll be in a position to be sell at a low price and still realize a comfortable profit. Remember that in the end, almost everything you buy will sell if it's realistically priced.

Are Your Prices Realistic?

This is going to sound paradoxical, but you can tell if you're assigning the right values to your merchandise by how much of it you're selling. Before you throw your hands up in exasperation, let's examine how you can determine realistic pricing as well as some other gauges you can apply.

Nothing Is Moving

Assuming you're getting some traffic through the shop and your mix of antiques is good, the most logical reason for not selling any of it is your pricing policy. You can't make that jump in reasoning too quickly, though, as natural cycles account for peaks and valleys in this, as in all other businesses. Before you start slashing prices, check with some other dealers. See how they're doing.

Things Are Selling Too Quickly

There's no such thing. I know that in some cases there's a tendency to feel that if things are selling more quickly than anticipated the prices might be too low. We all underprice things now and then, because none of us knows everything. Overall, though, if things are moving briskly and you're making a profit, you are probably pricing it just right. You *should* be selling more than everyone else after all.

Just Ask

Do some informal surveys. It's not necessary for you to be scientific about it. Put a box and little slips of paper, or a notebook, in your shop with a small sign. It might read: "I'm a new dealer. Help me out. How are my prices? I welcome all comments."

Hide Behind the Potted Plant

Skulk about in disguise? Blend into the background? You don't have to go quite that far, but if your shop is in a multidealer complex, you might not have a sense of how people are reacting to your displays and prices. You see only the end result in your sales.

On occasion, it will benefit you to station yourself outside your shop somewhere and to merely observe. Do mall patrons simply glance into

---

THE CUSTOMER COMMENT NOTEBOOK

You might want to make a notebook a permanent addition to your shop. Invite customers to leave comments and special requests for items they're seeking. Don't assume that every time you buy something to fulfill someone's wish list that they'll actually want it when it's available, but keep their names on file for future reference. I know dealers who don't have shops but have big, bulging notebooks full of collectors' names and numbers and their collecting passions.

your shop and amble on? If so, maybe you need to take another look at how you've decorated your shop or what you're stocking.

If they step in but double over with laughter while pointing at a price tag, you can bet you're overpricing your goods. Actually, their reactions are likely to be a lot more subtle than that, and that's when you should make your presence known. Explain that you're the owner and that you're curious about why they chose not to make a purchase.

It's possible that they just didn't find what they wanted, but if they're picking an item up, examining it closely, and then rejecting it, it could be that you're asking more than the "going" price.

How to Calculate Inventory Turnover

One of the most accurate measurements of the success of a retail business (aside from survival and longevity) is the turnover rate. As suggested by the term itself, it's a calculation that tells you how many times, within a given period, your inventory has been sold and replenished. It's of little use to know this information month to month but, at the end of your first year and each succeeding year, you should find this out. Fortunately, it doesn't take a computer or knowledge of higher math to determine turnover rate. Here's how it's done.

1. **Determine your beginning inventory.** (You'll need this figure at the end of the year for tax purposes, too.) The beginning inventory figure is the total value (at cost) of everything you've purchased for resale and have on hand on the first day of the business year. Let's use $8,000 as an example.
2. **Determine your closing inventory.** That's another figure you have to come up with, whether you do a turnover calculation or not. That number, of course, is the cost value of everything on hand at the end of the year. (This will also be the *beginning* inventory for the next year.) Let's say $10,000?
3. **Determine the cost of merchandise sold.** It gets a wee bit tricky here. This figure isn't just the amount of money you spent on new merchandise during the year, or the cost of the actual items you sold during that period. It's the *beginning inventory* ($8,000) plus all the purchases you've made since (including materials you used to improve them) — let's use a figure of $30,000 — minus *inventory at year's end* ($10,000).

   If you started with $8,000, bought $30,000, and have $10,000 left, the cost of merchandise sold during the year was $28,000. But you're not quite finished.

4. **Find your average inventory value.** This is easy. Add the beginning inventory ($8,000) to the closing inventory ($10,000): for this example, $18,000. To find the average, simply divide by 2, arriving at an average of $9,000. If you track your inventory by computer, or you're very conscientious, you probably know the value per month, in which case you can add all the monthly figures together and divide by 12.

5. **Figure your turnover rate.** Divide the *cost of inventory sold* ($28,000) by the *average inventory* ($9,000). The result is 3.1. That means you've turned your inventory a little over three times. Typically, a turnover rate of less than three isn't good, but for your first year in business, you haven't done bad at all.

Profit and Volume

Being aware of how people are reacting to your pricing, why they do or don't buy, and, ultimately, the speed at which you're selling and restocking your shop doesn't tell you much about the bottom line. For that reason, most dealers forgo this simple process and jump right to the line that reads net profit.

Knowing how much money you've made in a given period, without being aware of these other factors, can be misleading. Two shops, starting out roughly equal, might show identical profits at the end of the year. But let's assume that one shop had a turnover of four, while the other did two. You might think that since they profited equally, the fact that one shop had a better turnover is insignificant. Maybe one owner is satisfied with selling less but making more per item. What's wrong with that?

Odds are that in the long run the shop with double the turnover and smaller per-item profits will prosper, while the other business will slowly stagnate and die. In antiques stores and bakeries, stale stock will do you in. In my experience, the more business you do, the more you *will* do!

Discounting

I don't care if you're The World's Cheapest Antiques Dealer and you've priced things so they'll sell before the ink on the price tag dries: People will always ask you for a better price. To "freshen" your stock, it's also *sometimes* necessary to sell things at or below cost.

Bending

If you're required to be in your shop at all times, you'll face customers daily who insist on a lower price than what you've posted. Some dealers allow a little margin for this dickering and, admittedly, sometimes you'll have to bend because you've overpriced something. You thought you were being realistic, but the customer knows otherwise. In these cases, it's best to thank the customer for educating you and to yield to the request for a discount.

Standing Firm

Generally, if you assign reasonable prices in the first place in hopes of doing a high volume, you shouldn't hesitate to point this out to people: Invite them to check with other dealers. Explain that much of what you sell is bought by other dealers and that you've priced your merchandise so they can make a little profit, too.

Making Yourself Scarce

If you're in a group shop and don't have to spend time there as a condition of your rental agreement, you might question whether it's wiser to hang around or just periodically check up on and restock the booth. I've tried both, and I've talked to a lot of dealers who do one or the other. The only real reason to be in the shop at all times is so that customers will have someone to bargain with. And the outcome of that is a general lowering of prices.

If you're not there, they can't ask. It's too easy to succumb to the temptation to reduce something that, if priced fairly in the first place, doesn't have all that much room in it for haggling. So unless you're in it strictly for the camaraderie with other dealers and the opportunity to talk to the public — many are, and there's nothing wrong with that — it's better to be an absentee shopkeeper.

Let It Go

Obviously you can't afford to do this too often, but it's sometimes prudent to let a larger, more expensive item go at cost or — I hate saying this — at even less than what you paid for it. It's a fact of doing almost any type of retail business that sometimes, for the sake of generating cash to purchase new stock (or food!), you must sell things at a loss. It's better to take a small loss and rejuvenate your stock than to hold on to things that are just attracting dust, fingerprints, and disinterested glances. Because so many of the same faces pass through the same shops on a regular basis, I firmly believe that constantly changing the look of your shop does as much to help you sell as anything else you can do. So, on occasion, it's good to let go.

Was That Any Help?

I know that many of you were hoping to discover a secret method that dealers use for setting prices. When I was starting out, I struggled to find the right price for every item I placed in the shop, and I knew that the old, experienced hands had a better way of doing it. They just wouldn't tell me. After a few years, I realized that just being an "old, experienced hand" is the secret.

"Live and learn" isn't great advice in a how-to book, but at least you now have a head start on the learning part. Just remember what one old Vermont antiques dealer said when asked how much he got for an oak bedroom suite: "About half as much as I hoped but twice as much as I thought I would."

THE GOODY BOX

In my shops I always keep what I fondly call "my goody box." Items that have overstayed their welcome go in the box. These items haven't sold within what I consider to be a reasonable period; they might be slightly damaged or of poor quality, or may have been included with something more desirable at an auction and are just barely too good to throw away.

Attached to the box is a piece of paper that lists everything in it and the price for the box. The price is very low, but the condition of the sale is that the customer must take everything. Items are added, and the list updated, until it eventually sells.

The goody box serves the dual purpose of culling less desirable pieces and attracting return customers looking for a bargain. In some ways you might consider this similar to a "loss leader" for big discounters — that is, something priced not to make a profit but simply to get customers in the door.

▶20◀

some basics of business

Did you ever wonder why there have been plenty of television shows made about doctors, police officers, and attorneys, but never about accountants? Of course it's because that stuff bores most of us to death!

Thank goodness there are people who enjoy and devote their working lives to this type of endeavor, though. The business world literally turns on their efforts. Fortunately, operating a small business doesn't require that we become experts in accounting. You'll avoid a whole lot of trouble and worry down the road, though, if you can grasp a few principles and apply that knowledge consistently from the beginning.

If you're like me, you'll want to stick to the basics and keep the business end of the business as simple as possible. Since I'm the furthest thing from a lawyer or an accountant, I won't give you any legal or tax advice — except to find reputable legal and tax advisers. What I will tell you about are a few fundamental considerations.

Permit Me

Don't hang up that big "Antiques" sign or sell your first collectible without first obtaining all the necessary licenses and permits required by the state and local jurisdiction in which you're going to be operating. You could go to a lot of trouble and expense and end up being closed down before you get started. Find out what paperwork you need and get it.

Neighborhood Restrictions

Even if you live in a state or county that has few zoning laws and you plan to open a business at your residence, you might have restrictive *covenants* associated with your deed that ban the operation of any home businesses. If this is the case, and you ignore them, the local homeowners' association will start forming a posse. Get out that long, boring list of things the covenants say you can't do. Somewhere in there — along with not being allowed to burn your Christmas lights year-round — you might be barred from setting up a shop.

Zoning

If that's not the case, the city, town, township, borough, or county might have something to say about how you use your residential property. It could be as simple as paying a small fee to the local authorities for a zoning permit, or as complicated as going before a zoning board or presenting your request to a group of commissioners. Usually, a few calls to the courthouse, town hall, or another dealer will help you learn how to proceed.

That's one good point in favor of starting out in a group facility. You know it's okay to sell there. It might surprise you that even though the antiques center already has permission to operate, you too might be required to obtain a zoning permit to do business there. It's no big deal and doesn't require a complicated application process, but it is another fee and another piece of paper you need. Check with the courthouse.

Licenses

You can't open shop without a business license. The main purpose of this license, usually, is to inform the state that someone else out there will be collecting sales tax. It also informs the state that you have an inventory on which some states may levy tax. If you can operate in a variety of states, you might want to determine which one has the best deal for small retailers.

Perhaps your state doesn't impose a tax on sales. You still have to have a license to sell. Normally this license is very inexpensive and merely requires that you sign a request form. Once acquired, don't hesitate to use this license and the tax number you're assigned to obtain discounts from other merchants from whom you make business-related purchases.

A Set of Books

It pains me to say this, but you and I, despite all our other entrepreneurial duties (like hanging around in the back of an auction house, drinking coffee, and swapping lies with other dealers), must also become bookkeepers. Every business, no matter its size, requires a "set of books" into which inventory, purchase, sales, and other pertinent information is posted and kept as a permanent record. These records can be as sophisticated as computer-generated spreadsheets or as simple as a few spiral-bound notebooks.

Recording Your Inventory

In chapter 19, we talked about why it's important to know the value (cost) of your stock on hand, purchased, and sold. You, the state, and the IRS are all in agreement on this point. So the trick is — without devoting your life to the project — to come up with a simple, straightforward method of tracking this information. Here's what you need to know about every item that passes through your shop: (1) what it is, (2) when you bought it, (3) how much you paid for it, (4) when you sold it, and (5) how much you sold it for.

Now that's not all that much information, is it? The problem arises when you try to create a system of maintaining those facts that is simple, yet accurate and complete. Some dealers like to cram as much information as possible onto the price tag. They come up with elaborate codes that show at a glance not only the stock number and price, but the month and year of its purchase as well as what they paid for it.

INVENTORY/SALES JOURNAL

Date __1998__   Priced by __J. M.__   Sheet No. ____

Department ____ Extended by ____   Called by ____

Location ____   Examined by ____   Entered by ____

	ITEM NO.	DESCRIPTION	PURCHASED AT	SOLD AT	PURCHASE DATE	SOLD DATE
1	D990	Bed, single, walnut, Vict.	95 00	250 00	6-21	7-14
2	D991	Bed, 1940s, mahog, dbl.	25 00		6-21	
3	D992	Mirror, rect. 30x24, gold	75 00	155 00	6-21	8-11
4	D993	Roseville vase, Columbine, 9"	39 00	59 00	6-21	6-23
5	D994	Roseville, 5" vase, Carnelian	22 00	45 00	6-21	6-23
6	D995	Roseville, Rozane, unmk 8" vase	25 00	135 00	6-21	6-23
7	D996	1920s telephone, desk	5 00	30 00	7-1	9-12
8	D997	Print, boats, 10x14, unsgn.	2 00	20 00	7-1	9-9
9	D998	Print, Victorian, girl w/kitten	17 50		7-1	
10	D999	Print, C+I style, not signed	17 50	45 00	7-1	7-15
11	E1	Oak porch rocker	9 00	105 00	7-15	10-17
12	E2	Chair, mission style	35 00	165 00	7-15	7-30
13	E3	magazine rack, mahog.	3 00	27 00	7-15	8-5
14	E4	Book, medical, text 1889	.50	7 50	7-15	7-30
15						

Since you're going to have to put all this in a permanent record, I'd have to question the wisdom of duplicating it on a teeny-weeny price tag. If you just use a sequential stock number, beginning with #1 (what a radical idea!), then you can easily reference it in your inventory books, where all that other stuff, such as purchase price and date, is kept. If it concerns you that eventually you'll reach numbers up in the five-figure range, then consider adding a single letter, beginning with A. So your first item would be A1. When you've reached A999, switch to B and start over. This method will allow you to run through 999 items 26 times. That's nearly 26,000 items, which will hold you for a while. After item 25,974, you can move on to AA1, and so forth.

What's It Worth If It's Not Worth Anything?

In this odd commerce, unlike other retail trades, merchandise is sometimes purchased in lots as small as a cardboard carton or as large as a truck or houseful. The separate items in the lot can range from the relatively valuable to the totally worthless. How do you assign a dollar value to each item for inventory purposes? Since some things will be thrown or given away and the rest sold item by item, each item kept for resale must be assigned a value and a stock number.

BREAKING THE CODE

A dealer I know thought he was being very clever when he coded a lamp something like this: L#009a96CB. The "L" signified lamp, since he thought categorizing things would keep the stock numbers from getting too long. The numbers "009" explained that it was the ninth lamp purchased, the "a" that it was purchased in April, and the "96" referred to the year. The letters "CB" meant $30, his purchase price. In addition, the tag also had to contain a brief description of the merchandise, a dealer's code (because he was in a multidealer shop), and a selling price.

When he got his sales report, it read, "Lamp—$69." All the rest of that data were just too cumbersome for a busy clerk to record, so he had to go back to his inventory records, which contained identical details anyway!

Option #1. Some dealers prefer to divide the number of articles in the lot by the cost of the entire collection. For example, if the box contained twenty salable objects and cost five dollars, each piece is assigned an inventory value of twenty-five cents.

Option #2. You could also choose to allocate the entire five dollars to one item and make all the others equal zero dollars. The only problem with that method is when you need to take an actual inventory at year's end. If the five-dollar item has been sold and you're left with all these zeroes to add up, your inventory looks smaller than it actually is. The numbers work out better, though, since a smaller year-end inventory figure makes your profits look smaller, which is good for taxes. (That's because you add your beginning inventory to your cost of purchases and then subtract your ending inventory to come up with your cost of goods sold. That figure is subtracted from your total sales, equaling *profit.* A smaller ending inventory suggests greater costs and less profit.)

If, however, you sold all the no-value items and have the five-dollar stock on hand for inventory, profits look bigger. Bad for taxes. But wait. A larger inventory at end of year this year is a larger beginning inventory for next year, which, in theory, could decrease next year's apparent profits. Good then? Bad now?

I didn't do this to confuse you, but to show you how confusing it can become if you try to finagle things to make business appear better or worse, either to fool the tax man or yourself. I also did it to emphasize how important it is to keep records and to show that how they're kept can affect your bottom line.

Option #3. Whether you buy something, pick it up out of the junk pile, or someone gives it to you, it should still get an entry and an identifying number. I believe that assigning a realistic value to miscellaneous items works out best in the long run. For that reason, when you buy a five-dollar box, you'll probably end up with a variety of values totaling five dollars. Of course when you actually do get something for nothing, it's got to go in the book at no cost.

Summarize Systematically

If you do a large volume of business, your inventory record can become pretty awkward over time. For that reason you need to summarize this information periodically — at least annually when you do a physical inventory. You'll certainly want to track sales entries more frequently — each month, probably.

If possible, transfer all the information about whatever's on hand at inventory time to a new book at the beginning of each new year. A new section is okay, but an individual book for each year is better.

The Expense Ledger

This could end up being the most elaborate of your books. In this important record are documented all expenses associated with running your business, other than the cost of the merchandise you buy for resale. I suggest that you divide the ledger into sections dealing with the various categories of expenses.

The best place to get information about what constitutes an expense and how to categorize it is a Schedule C (with instructions), which is filed with your 1040 tax forms. Since the IRS wants you to keep accurate records, it'll provide you with these and other publications geared to small business owners. Don't wait until the end of the year to get them. They're free and surprisingly informative.

You can never have too much information in the expense ledger. It might not all turn out to be pertinent, but no one who faced an audit was ever told, "You've got way too many details here." If you buy a postage stamp for the business, log it. Log your mileage, gasoline, destinations, and auto repairs. Post your rent, the cost of having someone repair a chair, insurance, office supplies, and whatever else comes along. And save all those receipts!

Be specific when recording the cost of supplies. The can of paint used to spruce up the walls of your shop is classified differently from the can of paint that improves an item you're selling. Materials and supplies used for restoration increase the cost of the goods you sell. Of course this is picky! But since the tax forms differentiate between the two, so should you.

I Quit!

Don't let all this talk of books, ledgers, and journals frighten you off. Really, it's not all that bad. Start with some system you find comfortable and keep it up to date. The longer you put it off, the more difficult and overwhelming the task becomes. Carry little pocket-sized notebooks around with you. Transfer the notes from those to your permanent records, daily if possible.

Taxes

Although all the previous discussion sounds like "tax talk," don't forget that those records serve as valuable tools for analyzing the health of your business. We should mention a few more tax-related considerations while we're at it, though.

RECORD OF DISBURSEMENTS
Monthly Ledger of Expenses __January__

	MONTHLY ITEMS		Repair Supplies	Taxes (Sales)	Repair work	Parts for Antiques	Misc.	Insurance	Totals
DATE	EXPLANATION	AMOUNT							
1	Rent, Shop #1	160 00							160 00
2	Rent, Shop #2	150 00							150 00
3	C+H Supply, Lacquer+steel wool		31 00	1 86					32 86
4									
5									
6									
7	Crafter's Mall-paint		9 95	50					10 45
8									
9									
10									
11									
12	Hager Upholstery Shop, wingback				150 00				150 00
13									
14									
15									
16	Polishing work Brass lantern				30 00				30 00
17									
18	Sears, drill bits			42			7 00		7 42
19									
20	Copy Fast (copy flyer)			1 50			30 00		31 50
21									
22									
23									
24	Calls to suppliers						3 75		3 75
25									
26									
27	Lamp + lights (parts)					85 00			85 00
28									
29	Truck Insurance							650 00	650 00
30									
31									
	TOTAL	310 00	40 95	4 28	180 00	85 00	40 75	650 00	1310 98

Sales Tax

Unless you rent space in an antiques center where the management files sales tax for you, you're obligated to collect, file, and forward state sales tax on everything you sell, usually quarterly. Once you've applied for a license, you'll receive the necessary forms automatically.

Exempt Sales

If you sell to other dealers, your state might exempt them from paying taxes on items they purchase for resale. Check with your state tax office to determine how this works and what documentation you're required to keep. Remember that you're exempted from paying sales tax to other dealers, too.

Social Security Tax

If your antiques business is your only source of income or if less than the maximum annual contribution is deducted from your other income sources, you probably will have to file and pay self-employment (Social Security and Medicare) taxes. If you have an employee, you'll be faced with paying part of his or her Social Security taxes, too. Check with a professional or the IRS before you get involved with this.

Estimated Tax

It's not bad enough that you have to pay your income taxes, but when you're self-employed, the federal government wants you to do it quarterly and in advance! That means you've got to estimate how much you're going to make. About all the expert advice I have on this is, good luck!

State Income Tax

In most states these are based on your completed federal filing. You may not have to worry about filing quarterly taxes for the state, but if you don't, remember to hold something back to pay them annually.

Inventory Tax

As mentioned previously, some states levy a form of property tax that is based on a percentage of the value of your inventory at year's end. Where I live, I can do business easily in any of four states. Only one of them has such an inventory tax, so I don't have a shop there. Don't forget to check this detail when you get your license.

It's *Your* Business!

And, you'll have to mind it. I haven't presumed to try to tell you everything you need to know to operate it successfully. You've got to make a lot of personal informed choices. Here are a few more business considerations you should look into:

▸ **Take credit cards?** There's a fee. Check with your bank. It probably pays for itself in increased business.

▸ **Separate checking account?** Not absolutely necessary if you're small, but it's always a good idea to keep your household and business finances separated.

▸ **Insurance?** Your call, but you can suffer a significant loss if you're not insured. Antiques centers don't insure your losses. Are you insured for liability if someone is injured in your shop?

▸ **Partnerships?** Make it less costly to go into business, but be forewarned, they are seldom a good idea in this trade. You can start small on your own.

Closing Up

When I started this book I knew that I had to include a "business of business" chapter. I really struggled with the question of where to put it, though. It's sort of a shame to close with what, for most people, is the least interesting, most burdensome, part of the antiques business. It might make you forget about all the fun stuff we already learned.

Remember, if you didn't love antiques, you wouldn't have picked this book up in the first place. It's my sincere hope that my experience and your love of antiques combine to produce another successful dealer. Look in the back of the room at the next auction. I'll be the guy eating a hot dog, swapping lies with another bidder, and loving every minute of it. Will you join me?

glossary

Absentee bid Bid left with auctioneer for an item by bidder who cannot attend auction in person.

Adapter As used here, a threaded fitting that converts one size thread to another. Used in lamp conversion.

Airbrush A small, low-pressure paint sprayer.

Aniline A stain or dye that is mixed with a solvent.

Art pottery Decorative ceramic objects having some artistic, rather than purely utilitarian, purposes.

Auction house A permanent location at which auctions are held on a regular basis.

Barter An exchange of goods or labor for other goods or labor without an exchange of money.

Book value The supposed average value of antiques or collectibles as stated in various pricing-and-identification guidebooks.

Bridge lamp Floor lamp with a single, downward-pointing socket to which a shade is attached.

Buffing compound Abrasive in stick form applied to a moving buffing wheel; used to polish metals.

Buyer's premium Percentage paid by buyer at auctions in addition to amount bid.

Consignment sale Auction at which items are consigned for sale by several people paying a commission to the auctioneer.

Co-op As used here, a multidealer antiques store where dealers must contribute time and work.

Covenants Deed restrictions that govern property usage.

Crazing Fine lines that develop over time in the glaze of a ceramic object.

Dowel (or dowel pin) A wooden pin used in furniture construction to hold pieces together.

End cutter A type of pliers made for cutting flush with a surface.

Ephemera Term used for paper collectibles.

Epoxy A two-part substance that when mixed together forms a strong, durable material for repairing various materials.

Estate sale Auction at which possessions of a deceased person are sold.

Exempt sales Sales that are exempted from state sales tax because they are made to dealers for resale.

Faux (or faux finish) A technique used to make one material look like another (wood to marble, etc.)

Feather painting Use of an actual feather to decorate with paint.

Finishing nail A small-head nail to secure wood.

Flea market Gathering of antiques, collectibles, or other merchandise dealers in one spot.

Foam board A stiff paper and plastic-foam material used to form the backing for pictures.

Framer's pliers A tool for inserting brads into picture frames; also called a brad setter.

Furniture powder A powdered colorant mixed with a solvent to make a stain.

Gesso The plaster/glue substance that covers picture frames.

Glaze An opaque color; also the kiln-fired finish of a ceramic piece.

Graining Simulating the grain patterns found in wood; a faux-finishing process.

Grosgrain A type of ribbed ribbon used in sewing and edging of lampshades.

Group shop An antiques store that has a number of spaces rented to individual dealers.

House number Bidder's number assigned to the auctioneer.

Inventory The merchandise kept for resale; also the actual process of checking and listing that merchandise, usually on a yearly basis.

Jardiniere A large flowerpot, usually made to sit on a matching pedestal.

Jeweler's rouge A fine, buffing compound.

Knock down To end bidding; from use of gavel to announce item sold at an auction.

Lath Thin wooden strips.

Loss leader Something sold by a retailer at or near cost for the purposes of attracting customers.

Lot A number of items sold at auction as a group; sometimes items in boxes sold as "box lots."

Mall As used here, a large building or buildings having spaces rented to a number of antiques dealers.

Marbleizing A faux-finishing technique that simulates marble.

Marriage Two or more pieces of furniture made into one.

Migrating smalls Small objects at auctions that are moved about by bidders to confuse other bidders.

Mining the ads Looking for antiques in classified ads by keying on particular words.

Mint Term used to describe an object that is in perfect, or seemingly unused, condition.

Mogul socket The large, central socket that holds a big-based, three-way bulb in a floor lamp.

Muriatic acid An acid primarily used as a cleaning agent. Useful in removing cement residue, calcium and rust deposits, and tarnish.

Nipple A threaded pipe used in lighting and lamps.

Patina Finish acquired through years of handling or a finish applied to something to simulate age.

Philatelist A collector of postage stamps.

Picker One who attends auctions or buys antiques from other sources to resell to antiques dealers.

Picture wire A strong, multistrand wire used for hanging heavy objects, such as pictures and mirrors.

Pontil A metal rod that holds a glass object being blown; the pontil mark is the mark left by it.

Pouncing A method of using a nearly dry brush to spread paint into corners and crevices.

Preview Time allotted to examine merchandise before an auction.

Prints Term used to describe lithographs or other printed artwork, as opposed to handpainted or drawn.

Provenance The history of an antique: who owned, when made, who made, etc.

Raffia A natural fiber available from craft stores.

Reserve Predetermined lowest price at which an item can be sold at auction.

Schedule C The tax form used by dealers to file the profit or loss from business.

Screw eye A type of screw having a closed loop instead of a head. Used for hanging framed items with wire.

Shard A piece of broken pottery.

Shot Small pellets of lead or steel.

Shotting Cleaning a bottle by shaking with shot and detergent.

Shows Gatherings of antiques or collectibles dealers for the purpose of displaying, buying, and selling.

Signature (or signed) Artist's name or manufacturer's imprint on an object.

Silvering The reflective coating on a mirror's back.

Sizing A solution applied to a surface such as a wall or the inside of a trunk to provide better adhesion of wallpaper, and easier removal.

Slag glass A swirled, multicolored glass used as bases and ornament on lamps and other objects.

Slip seat Removable seat of a wooden chair.

Smalls Any small collectible object.

Sponging Application of paint with sponges or similar material.

Spot putty (or glazing) Sold in tubes at auto supply stores for filling fine scratches in body work prior to painting; used here in pottery restoration.

Stacked frame Sometimes called composite, or nested, frames; several individual frames making up one.

Stretcher The brace that extends between the legs of furniture.

Stripper A solution used to dissolve and remove paint and other finishes, like lacquer or varnish.

Sweat equity Profits earned through one's own efforts to improve an object.

Tack rag A rag impregnated with a sticky substance; used to remove dust from a wood surface prior to application of a finish.

Turnover (or turnover rate) The number of times inventory is sold and replenished.

Uno (or Uno thread) The most common thread size of the end of a light socket onto which a shade can be screwed.

Usage mark Small imperfections that indicate an item (usually glass) is old and has been used.

Vase cap A cap, usually brass, that fits over the opening of a vase to convert it to a lamp.

Veining In marbleizing, creating the irregular lines normally present in real marble.

Veneer Very thin sheets of real wood.

Verdigris A natural or applied blue-green finish normally associated with brass, copper, or bronze.

Victorian Pertaining to style or age of an object that dates from mid- to late nineteenth century.

Washing soda Similar to baking soda but used as a laundry additive.

Wet-and-dry (or wet-or-dry) Type of sandpaper designed to be used with or without water as a lubricant.

Zoning Laws governing the use of property.

suggested reading and references

Books

Demoyed, Trudie. *Calligraphy for Beginners*. London: Savitri Books, Ltd., 1994. *Nice beginners' manual for the art of calligraphy.*

Fields, Louis. *Bookkeeping Made Simple*. Revised by Richard R. Gallagher. New York: Doubleday, 1990. *This book makes this onerous task relatively simple.*

Grotz, George. *The Furniture Doctor*. New York: Doubleday, 1976. *A classic of furniture repair. Mr. Grotz is one of the best for simple fixes.*

Hood, Timothy. *Mastering Calligraphy*. North Dighton, MA: JG Press, Inc., 1996. *Another handy reference if you want to make special price tags.*

Huxford, Sharon and Bob, eds. *Schroeder's Antiques Price Guide*. New York: Collector Books, annual. *A must-have pricing-and-identification guide for all dealers. Very complete.*

Jackson, Albert. *The Antique Care and Repair Handbook*. New York: Knopf, 1984. *Covers some ground that I didn't.*

Johnson, Kay, Olivia Elton Barrett, and Mary Butcher. *Chair Seating*. London: Dryad Press, Ltd., 1988. *A nicely illustrated how-to of caning, rush, and other seat-weaving techniques.*

Ketchum, William, Jr. *Auction!* New York: Sterling, 1980. *If you want an entire book about auctions, this is it.*

Kirshel, George, and Patricia Kirshel. *Start, Run and Profit from Your Own Home-Based Business*. New York: John Wiley and Sons, Inc., 1991. *An excellent start-up book for small businesses.*

Kovel, Ralph. *Kovel's Antiques and Collectibles Fix-It Source Book*. New York: Crown, 1990. *The name Kovel is synonymous with antiques, so you can depend on a Kovel book to provide you with good information.*

Kovel, Ralph. *Kovel's Guide to Selling, Buying, and Fixing Your Antiques*. New York: Crown, 1995. *Another good Kovel book.*

Kovel, Ralph, and Terry Kovel, eds. *Kovel's Antiques and Collectibles Price List*. New York: Crown, annual. Updated periodically. *Standard pricing-and-identification.*

McCloud, Kevin. *Kevin McCloud's Complete Book of Paint and Decorative Techniques*. New York: Simon & Schuster, 1996. *A wonderful source of information for novices and experts alike. Lots of decorative tricks and information on finishes and colors.*

Plant, Tim. *Painted Illusions: A Creative Guide to Painting Murals and Trompe L'oeil Effects.* Topsfield, MA: Salem House, 1988. *You might not be this artistic, but you'll enjoy looking at the pictures and you might learn something.*

Rinker, Harry, ed. *Warman's Americana and Collectibles.* Iola, WI: Krause Publications, 1997. Updated regularly. *An excellent reference for prices and identification of collectibles that were mass-produced and made in the twentieth century. This is where a lot of the money is made. (Ellen T. Schroy took over the editing of this valuable resource in 1998.)*

Taubes, Frederick. *Antique Finishing for Beginners.* New York: Watson Guptill, 1972. *As it says, for beginners. Good information here.*

Periodicals

There are a number of monthly, and even weekly, newspapers dealing with the trade. Each region of the country has several, and being regional, will keep you informed of what's happening in the business locally. Complimentary copies are usually available at larger antiques centers.

In the East we have widely circulated papers like the *Antiques and Auction News* published by Joel Slater Publications, P.O. Box 500, Mt. Joy, PA 17552, and *The MidAtlantic Antiques Magazine*, P.O. Box 908, Henderson, NC 27536. I haven't attempted to list the many regional newsletters, but there are a few nationally distributed newsletters of interest. For instance:

Antique Week, P.O. Box 90, Knightstown, IN 46148. Publishes 51 issues a year. *Check to see if it has a version for your region of the country. Full of good articles, auctions, books, shows, and antiques for sale.*

Kovel's On Antiques and Collectibles, Box 22200, Beachwood, OH 44122. *Up-to-the-minute information about what's happening in the world of antiques. A good source for both collectors and dealers.*

Warman's Today's Collector, 700 E. State St., Iola, WI 54990. *Like most periodicals, it contains a lot of ads, but unlike many, is filled with well-written, informative articles and photographs.*

Helpful Information from the IRS

The Internal Revenue Service not only wants you to make money and pay taxes, but it would like to help you avoid mistakes in recordkeeping and filing your returns. Since all the help it offers is free, why not take advantage of it?

Publication 454A is a package of forms and publications of interest to people in, or about to enter, small business. Call 1-800-829-3676 to request it.

Also, the IRS has a program called STEP, which stands for *Small Business Tax Education Program* that offers free seminars and educational programs at locations scattered around the country. You might be able to take advantage of one near you. Call 1-800-829-1040 to find out.

sources: suppliers and manufacturers

This is not a complete list, by any means. There are manufacturers big and small, wholesalers, and retailers all over the country who specialize in restorer's merchandise. And of course your local hardware store, paint store, and home supply sellers carry much of what you need. Only toll-free phone numbers are included.

Abatron Inc.
5501 95th Avenue
Kenosha, WI 53144
800-445-1754
Moldmaking and casting compounds

Badger Air-Brush Co.
9128 W. Belmont Avenue
Franklin Park, IL 60131
Airbrushes, equipment, and compressors

B & P Lamp Supply, Inc.
843 Old Morrison Highway
McMinnville, TN 37110
800-822-3450
Lamp and lighting parts and supplies

C & H Supply
5431 Mountville Road
Adamstown, MD 21710
Lacquers, strippers and stripping supplies, chair weaving, finishes, trunk and furniture hardware, buffing and polishing, antique telephone, furniture powders, stains, aniline dyes, and other trade goods

Charolette Ford Trunks, Ltd.
Box 536
Spearman, TX 79081
800-553-2649
Trunk restoration materials, handles, loops, drawbolts, etc.

Collector Books
P.O. Box 3009
Paducah, KY 42002-3009
800-626-5420
More than two hundred price-and-identification guidebooks on antiques and collectibles

DeBono Inc.
1165 Montauk Highway
P.O. Box 2097
East Patchogue, NY 11772
Reasonable and well-made line of lampshades

de Sherbinin Products
P.O. Box 63
Hawleyville, CT 06440-0063
800-458-0010
Lamp and lighting parts, shades, globes, wire, and tools

Harbor Freight
3491 Mission Oaks Boulevard
Camarillo, CA 93011-6010
800-423-2567
Good source of inexpensive and moderately priced hand and power tools, gloves, sandpaper, etc.

Kwick Kleen Industrial Solvents, Inc.
P.O. Box 905
Vincennes, IN 47591-0905
800-475-9144
or
P.O. Box 1718
Dover, DE 19901
800-648-1311
*Professional stripping supplies, tools, and
refinishing products*

The Lamp Shop
54 South Main Street
P.O. Box 36
Concord, NH 03302-0036
*Lampshade making and covering materials,
patterns, instructional booklets, and related
parts*

Masters Magic Products, Inc.
Highway 6
Perry, TX 76677
800-548-6583
*Strippers, stains, veneers, hardware and more
than 2,000 products for the refinisher,
restorer*

Midwest Lamp Parts Co.
3534 N. Spaulding Avenue
Chicago, IL 60618
*Lamp and lighting parts, shades, globes,
wire, and tools*

Patina Finishes & Copper Coats, Inc.
3486 Kurtz, Suite 102
San Diego, CA 92110
1-800-882-7004
*Solutions and coatings to add "antique"
patina to metal surfaces*

Rejuvenation Lamp & Fixture Co.
1100 S.E. Grand Avenue
Portland, OR 97214
*High-quality reproduction lighting and glass
shades*

Reliable Finishing Products, Inc.
1330 Louis Avenue
Elk Grove, IL 60007
800-717-1776
*That wonderful V. S. Vinyl Sealer & Finish,
other professional refinishing and stripping
supplies, tools, cleaners, and polishes*

Renovator's
P.O. Box 2515
Conway, NH 03818-2515
800-659-2211
*Reproduction house and furniture hardware,
chair seats, lighting, glass globes, reproduction plumbing fixtures*

Van Dyke's Restorers
4th Avenue and 6th Street
P.O. Box 278
Woonsocket, SD 57385
800-558-1234
*Upholstery tools and supplies, lighting parts,
refinishing products; curved, bowed, and
bubble glass, house and furniture hardware,
restorer's tools, artist's brushes, airbrushes,
veneers; furniture legs, seats, and other diffi-
cult-to-find reproduction replacement parts,
such as icebox hinges and "Hoosier" cabinet
accessories; and framing supplies*

The Woodworker's Store
4365 Willow Drive
Medina, MN 55340
800-279-4441
*Woodworking tools, hardware, finishes,
veneers, kits, framing supplies, glues, fillers,
fasteners, trunk parts, and clock movements*

WSI Distributors
425 N. Main Street
St. Charles, MO 63301
800-447-9974
*Brass hardware, rocker parts, veneers, furni-
ture parts, wax*

index

r

other storey titles
you will enjoy

Be Your Own Home Decorator: Creating the Look You Love without Spending a Fortune, by Pauline B. Guntlow. How to maximize space and inexpensively customize kitchens, bedrooms, living rooms, and baths with charm and taste. 144 pages. Paperback. ISBN 0-88266-945-1.

Buying and Selling Antiques, by Sara Pitzer and Don Cline. A professional guide to identifying antiques that retain value, auctions and auctioneers, and starting a business with a minimal investment. 112 pages. Paperback. ISBN 0-88266-406-9.

Decorative Stamping: Hundreds of Projects for Your Home, by Sasha Dorey. A step-by-step guide to decorating nearly any flat surface around the home. Includes paint selection, purchasing stamps, and how to apply a design. 96 pages. Cloth. ISBN 0-88266-809-9.

HomeMade: 101 Easy-to-Make Things for Your Garden, Home, or Farm, by Ken Braren and Roger Griffith. Complete, easy-to-follow directions for several projects, including a lawn chair, compost bin, and movable shed. 176 pages. Paperback. ISBN 0-88266-103-5.

Reviving Old Houses: Over 500 Low-Cost Tips & Techniques, by Alan Dan Orme. Practical advice on roofs, walls, masonry, glazing, insulation, plumbing, doors, stairs, floors, exteriors, and more. 180 pages. Paperback. ISBN 0-88266-563-4.

The Rummager's Handbook: Finding, Buying, Cleaning, Fixing, Using, and Selling Secondhand Treasures, by R. S. McClurg. Hundreds of tips and advice on finding sales, understanding prices, determining value, bargaining, and taking items home. 160 pages. Paperback. ISBN 0-88266-894-3.

These and other Storey Books are available
at your bookstore, farm store, garden center, or directly from
Storey Books, Schoolhouse Road, Pownal, Vermont 05261,
or by calling 800-441-5700. www.storey.com